THE WOW FACTOR

INSIDER STYLE SECRETS

for EVERY BODY
and EVERY BUDGET

THE WOW FACTOR

by **JACQUI STAFFORD**
Fashion Editor and
TV Style Expert

INSIDER STYLE SECRETS
for EVERY BODY
and EVERY BUDGET

published by
GOTHAM BOOKS

design by
EIGHT AND A HALF, NYC
8 1/2

GOTHAM BOOKS
PUBLISHED BY PENGUIN GROUP

Penguin Group (USA) Inc., 375 Hudson Street, New York, New York 10014, USA

Penguin Group (Canada), 90 Eglinton Avenue East, Suite 700, Toronto,
Ontario M4P 2Y3, Canada (a division of Pearson Penguin Canada Inc.);
Penguin Books Ltd, 80 Strand, London WC2R 0RL, England; Penguin Ireland,
25 St Stephen's Green, Dublin 2, Ireland (a division of Penguin Books Ltd);
Penguin Group (Australia), 707 Collins Street, Melbourne, Victoria 3008, Australia
(a division of Pearson Australia Group Pty Ltd); Penguin Books India Pvt Ltd,
11 Community Centre, Panchsheel Park, New Delhi – 110 017, India; Penguin Group
(NZ), 67 Apollo Drive, Rosedale, Auckland 0632, New Zealand (a division of Pearson
New Zealand Ltd); Penguin Books (South Africa), Rosebank Office Park, 181 Jan Smuts
Avenue, Parktown North 2193, South Africa; Penguin China, B7 Jiaming Center,
27 East Third Ring Road North, Chaoyang District, Beijing 100020, China

Penguin Books Ltd, Registered Offices:
80 Strand, London WC2R 0RL, England
Published by Gotham Books,
a member of Penguin Group (USA) Inc.

First printing, February 2013
1 3 5 7 9 10 8 6 4 2

LIBRARY OF CONGRESS CATALOGING-IN-PUBLICATION DATA
has been applied for.

ISBN 978-1-592-40773-6

Printed in the United States of America
Set in Amasis, Giorgio and Knockout.

DESIGN BY EIGHT AND A HALF, BROOKLYN, NY
ILLUSTRATIONS BY DANIELLE KROLL

FOR MY
DELICIOUSLY
NAUGHTY
CHARLOTTE

CONTENTS

HELLO, DARLINGS!

If you've ever wondered just what it is about some women that make all eyes follow them, then this no-nonsense style book is for you. You see, some people just have "it," that indefinable something you can never quite put your finger on: The WOW FACTOR. They're the ones who always manage to look effortlessly stylish, pulled-together, and, well…WOW! But if you think they were born with it—think again. I firmly believe that you don't have to be rich or skinny to be fabulous, so I'm going to spell out the simple, time-tested insider secrets to looking like a knockout— and it's got absolutely nothing to do with following fashion trends or being a size 0.

Enter: *The WOW FACTOR*. This book cuts through the clutter and gets down to the real nitty-gritty of what makes you look gorgeous. My non–fashion person's fashion book will give you practical, insider fashion advice in this (very often) unrealistic fashion and beauty world. I'm going to take the guesswork, mystery, and fear out of your wardrobe and bathroom cabinet— and have you turning heads for decades. I'm going to show you what to wear when you truly think you've got nothing in your closet. I'll give you the honest, down-to-earth scoop on what really helps hide your problem areas and accentuates the parts of your body that you love.

Super stylish dad

Me with my twin sister

See? A fashionista in the making

So if you've ever felt baffled and overwhelmed by the fashion and beauty industries, I know exactly how you feel. Maybe you've thumbed through a glossy magazine filled with images of stunning, long-limbed beauties and wondered, Why do they look like that—and I don't? But the truth is that the fashion industry never reveals what really goes on behind the scenes. You'll rarely hear the truth about the time and effort it takes to make a cover model look "effortless." (The fact is that every shot you see has taken a small army of people to create, months of planning, weeks of discussion, days of shooting, and all kinds of insider secrets and tricks that I'm going to share with you.)

I'm going to tell you how to really look great. You'll learn how to figure out your body shape so shopping trips are easier, and learn why just a few simple accessories will take you from blah to brilliant. I'll share the trends to ignore and the ones to embrace, plus I'll tell you about the secrets tricks to shave off years and inches. Also, I'll teach you the secrets to looking wealthy (even if you're not).

Even before I did this for a living, I was a fashionista—a trait inherited from my dad. (See how fabulously stylish he was?) Always dapper with Italian silk socks and a vividly colored pocket square peeping

*How to add 10 lbs
with just a sweater*
↓

*What was I thinking
in this outfit?*
↓

That hair! Yikes!
↓

out from an exquisitely tailored suit. But along my own journey to becoming a style expert—and thousands of make-overs later on women just like you—I've made some pretty laughable fashion mistakes. (I actually thought I looked good in the middle image above. Pity no one pointed out how those baggy mid–calf length pants drew attention to my chunky legs.) I've had my own struggles with weight and made some classic fashion disasters before I figured out exactly what looks great on me and what doesn't. (Here's a particularly enlightening example of what *not* to do: Don't wear an oversized, chunky cable-knit unless you want to look…oversized and chunky, exactly like me in this dreadful patterned sweater (top left). And I've also made some less-than-flattering hairstyle decisions. (See above pic. Need I say more.)

So stifle your giggles, and let's get to work. Don't waste another precious second of your life putting off your own WOW FACTOR. For every woman who's ever been frustrated and sweaty in a dressing room, lusted after shoes that she can't afford, or flipped through the pages of magazine and despaired about her thighs, this book is my love letter to you.

Get ready, my darlings—because I'm about to tell you...*everything*.

FIGURE OUT FASHION

LOVE ONLY THE CLOTHES THAT LOVE YOU BACK

There are just five body shapes, and I guarantee you'll recognize yourself within one. And while your weight might fluctuate, you're born with your shape. A triangle won't magically turn into a rectangle, I'm afraid. Stand in front of a full-length mirror in natural light, naked. ("Naked?" I can hear you scream. "Has she lost her mind?") Take an honest look: are your shoulders broad and powerful, or narrow and slender? Your waist: is there a definite curve, or are you straight up and down? Your arms: are they bulky, or can you fit your entire hand around your bicep? Is your tummy fairly flat, or full and womanly? Look not just at the parts of your body you loathe, but more important, find the parts you love—because that's what we're going to highlight. I don't care if you're a size 2 or a 20: I'll help you be smart about what you choose to wear. Don't waste another dime on those expensive fashion mistakes that look great…on someone else.

I've created five silhouettes: Sunglasses, Fragrance Bottle, Heart Pendant, Cocktail Ring, and Lipstick. When you see the icon for your body shape next to an item, you'll know it'll work specifically for you. So turn the page to take one step closer to WOW…

…AND SEE WHY YOUR BODY SHAPE
IS THE ONLY THING THAT MATTERS. REALLY.

WHICH SHAPE ARE YOU?

Here's the thing: Figure out your body shape, and you can create your best body imaginable. You see, the fashion industry is obsessed with size, but what matters most is your shape. The number on the tag means nothing (even if that number is a double 0) if you don't wear what flatters your body's natural proportions.

SUNGLASSES

BALANCED CURVES ON TOP AND BOTTOM

Turn to page

16

FRAGRANCE BOTTLE

SMALLER ON TOP, BIGGER ON BOTTOM

Turn to page

24

HEART PENDANT

BIGGER ON TOP, SMALLER ON BOTTOM

Turn to page

32

COCKTAIL RING

A LITTLE MORE IN THE MIDDLE

Turn to page

40

LIPSTICK

FAIRLY STRAIGHT UP AND DOWN

Turn to page

48

SUNGLASSES

{ BALANCED CURVES ON TOP AND BOTTOM }

ARE YOU SHAPED LIKE SUNGLASSES?

☐ Do you have fairly balanced shoulders and hips?

☐ Do you like to show off your waist?

☐ Do you have shapely legs?

☐ Do you wear the same size top and bottom?

If you checked at least three of these questions, my darling, you're a pair of Sunglasses!

MOST WOMEN THINK YOU'RE REALLY LUCKY.
You've got a fairly balanced top half, a defined waistline, and womanly hips. Sounds good, right? But the challenge—and I know, since I've worked with a gazillion women with your shape—is showcasing your slender waistline without making your torso look short. You have an enviable shape, but a few false moves and you could easily end up making yourself look heavier. It's beyond fabulous to have a waistline like yours, but we're going to work on assuring that you've got the perfect symmetry above and below it. Let's highlight those curves, but let's also make sure everything looks classy, sophisticated, and WOW!

SUNGLASSES SECRETS
Check out these pages throughout the book for fabulous tips on how to WOW.

117   119   121   123   125   156   162

YOUR BEST WOW FIT

WEEKEND

Got something in a neutral shade? Add a splash of vibrancy with a bright bag and strappy flats to complete the outfit.

BELTED DRESS

It's hard to find something more flattering than a belted dress to showcase your hourglass figure, as it makes you look pulled together and polished all in one go. (In winter, add knee-high boots and slip on a waist-nipping jacket.) Look for V-necks that allow for a supportive bra and hint at your bust without overexposing it. A belt around the middle will draw attention to your curvaceous waist without clinging to it.

EVENING

FORM-FITTING DRESS

Even though you're in perfect proportion, exposing less flesh is far sexier than giving it all away at first glance. A fuller-coverage, figure-hugging dress with a hint of stretch will skim over your curves without revealing your boobs and bum. Keep the length of the dress just at the knee—any shorter with this silhouette and you run the risk of looking trashy. Avoid boring black: everyone else will be wearing it. Yawn.

Your body, that dress. Keep your evening accessories conservative.

SWIMSUIT

*In between sizes?
Halter styles and side
ties adjust to fit.*

CURVE-HUGGING BIKINI

Go for enough coverage on the top half to
contain your bust (spillage = unsexy) and
look for bottoms with a slightly higher
cut leg to make you look longer and leaner.

INSIDE SCOOP

If you tie the side strings of your
bikini slightly toward the front
of your hips, rather than exactly at
the side, you'll visually trim off inches
no matter what shape you are.

COAT

BELTED TRENCH

A fitted, belted style in a lighter-weight fabric
is key to highlighting the curve of your figure,
and a plunging V-neck points to the narrow-
ness of your waistline. Go for a slightly flared
style that mimics your classic hourglass, and
keep away from oversized, boxy coats that hide
your shape. A bold collar adds drama, places
the focus on your upper half, and makes your
waist look teeny tiny in comparison.

WARDROBE ESSENTIALS

1

FITTED TEE
Go for a scoop neck
or a deep V style.
Invest in a stack
of slim-fitting tees,
which are great for
layering, in every
shade imaginable.
Look for ones that
are long enough to
tuck into pants so
they highlight your
natural waistline.
The insider way to
wear a weekend tee:
the "half tuck"—a
nonchalant half-in,
half-out tuck that
gives you that "effort-
less" look.

2

BELTED DRESS
Fitted or flowing, it
needs to be belted.
Choose dresses that
follow your natural
waistline rather than
shapeless sacks that
engulf you. Look for
ones with slender
belts or elasticated
waists. (Billowy, bell
sleeves are a fabulous
fashion fix if you don't
like your arms.)

3

PENCIL SKIRT
A structured skirt in
a stiffer fabric plays
up good legs; add
sheer or printed
hosiery to draw even
more attention to
your feminine shape.
Keep your top tucked
in to show off your
waist. Pair a pencil
skirt with a fitted
button-down and
a blazer for work,
or a blousy peasant
top and knee-high
boots for a more
casual look.

4

**HALTER-NECK
TOP**
Halters showcase
gorgeous shoulders.
Invest in a good
strapless bra to lift up
the bust (so you don't
look short-waisted)
and pair with a
plainer bottom half
like a simple black
skirt or pants. My
style rule: lots of
exposed flesh up top
requires more cover-
age below.

Love this!

CURVE-HUGGING STRAIGHT DRESS

Your hourglass shape can pull off a structured, sleek sheath dress that might cling in all the wrong places on anyone else. Keep the length to the knee; any longer and you risk looking like a School Marm.

BELTED CARDIGAN

Belted cardigans show off your naturally slender waist. Add a silky skirt or wide leg pants and a brightly colored shirt to soften the effect. Keep away from chunky, menswear-inspired cableknits that add unwanted pounds. Instead, look for form-fitting lightweight knits.

SKINNY CARGO PANTS

A curvy shape can carry off a straighter, tighter silhouette like slimline cargos. Pair with a fitted tee and bold, chunky heels for a date night, or a cardi and Parisian-chic ballet flats for weekends.

CROPPED LEATHER JACKET

Major curves can carry off a butter-soft leather jacket. Look for unexpected shades instead of biker black—camel, red, or tan work as neutrals and go with just about everything. Counter the masculine shape by keeping the rest of your outfit ultra-feminine— use as a keep-warm topper for flirtacious skirts or dresses.

STYLIST RULES TO SWEAR BY

BELTED PIECES DRAW ATTENTION
TO THE NARROWNESS OF YOUR WAIST
and highlight your hourglass shape.

FITTED DRESSES AND TOPS THAT
SKIM OVER YOUR BODY
are far more flattering than shapeless pieces
that hide your figure.

YOUR ULTRA-FEMININE BODY SHAPE
CAN GET AWAY WITH MENSWEAR-INSPIRED JACKETS,
which look less masculine on super-curvy you.

DON'T WEAR BOXY,
SQUARE-LOOKING PIECES.
They just hide your waistline.

DON'T WEAR OVERTLY SEXY TOPS.
Less skin on display is always classier.

AND DON'T EVEN THINK ABOUT WEARING
LOOSE-FITTING PANTS
that drown your bottom half.

THE BOTTOM LINE:
HIGHLIGHT YOUR WAIST, CELEBRATE YOUR CURVES, AND STEER CLEAR OF SHAPELESS, BAGGY CLOTHES.

FRAGRANCE BOTTLE

{ SMALLER ON TOP, BIGGER ON BOTTOM }

ARE YOU SHAPED LIKE A FRAGRANCE BOTTLE?

☐ Do you think you look "bottom-heavy"?

☐ Do you find pants that fit your hips but gape at the waist?

☐ Do you need a whole size bigger on your bum?

☐ Do you have a flat tummy and slim waist?

If you checked at least three of these questions, my darling, you're a Fragrance Bottle!

IF YOUR HIPS, THIGHS, AND BUM WERE JUST A TEENY BIT SMALLER, THEN YOU'D BE PERFECT, RIGHT?

I know—thus is the plight of the Fragrance Bottle. (I feel the same way since I've got the same shape, my darlings.) You probably never have a problem finding tops that fit, but usually need to go up a size or two to fit your butt (so annoying). And no matter how much weight you lose, it never seems to come off your bum or thighs. I get it. But think about your slender arms, your elegant back, and your flat tummy (plus your boobs don't look too bad, either). Yes, you might want to hide your voluptuous bottom with darker colors, and yes, you may want to steer clear of skirts that cling to your thighs. But, my dear Fragrance Bottle, you can wear so many gorgeous tops, and the world can't wait to see how stunning you'll look in them.

FRAGRANCE BOTTLE SECRETS

Check out these pages throughout the book for fabulous tips on how to WOW.

117   119   121   123   125   156   162

WEEKEND

All eyes upward!
Big bum?
What big bum?

PATTERNED TUNIC TOP WITH DARK WASH JEANS

Find a pair of dark-colored, polished-looking jeans, and partner them with a boldly printed top that covers your butt. When it comes to jeans (and other casual pants), look for cuts that fit snugly through the hips and thighs, and then have a subtle flare below the knee to balance your bottom half.

EVENING

STRAPLESS DRESS WITH A WIDE, FLARED BOTTOM

Don't you love how that fancy flare completely conceals hips and thighs? (For all people know, you have a tiny, pert little bum hidden under there!) Your best evening look is a cocktail dress that cinches you in at the waistline, then falls gently away from the body. A strapless or broad neckline will make your hips and thighs look smaller in comparison.

Add the finishing touches: keep your evening accessories in the same color family.

SWIMSUIT

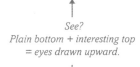

See?
Plain bottom + interesting top
= eyes drawn upward.

BOLD AND EMBELLISHED TOP WITH A SIMPLE BOTTOM

Distract from your lower half with an eye-catching neckline, like a deep V or a one-shoulder style. Look for straps that sit at the widest part of your shoulders to create the illusion of a V-shape for an instantly slimmer looking bottom half. Bikini separates featuring bold prints and colors, detailing and embellishment on the top, paired with a solid, simple bottom will downplay wide hips.

COAT

KNEE-LENGTH WITH AN OVERSIZED COLLAR

An exaggerated collar helps add welcome width to your top half, and will divert attention from your heavier lower half. Go for a longer-length style that hits the knee, and look for one with a slight A-line flare from the waistline to help balance fuller hips and create an hourglass silhouette.

WARDROBE ESSENTIALS

1

2

3

4

A-LINE DRESS
Go for dresses with a gentle A-line flare from the waist down. A-lines will skim over your hips and bum to brilliantly conceal your bottom half. Get one that hits just at the knee; any longer and it risks making you look dumpy.

SLIMLINE BLAZER
A chocolate, navy, or charcoal jacket will glide over your torso and completely cover your butt. Make sure it hits at the top of the thigh (no shorter!) and you can wear it over just about everything: a white shirt for work with a knee-length skirt, or with the sleeves pushed up over a fitted tank and boot-cut jeans for weekends.

LEGGINGS
Leggings? With my legs? But the secret lies in the color (black, no bright or light shades) and in adding an oversized, slouchy, thigh-skimming (not belted, not short) boy-friend sweater and ballet flats. The result? A bigger top half and skinnier bottom. Oh, and it's a stylish, fuss-free weekend look.

COLORED SCARF
The brighter the better. Embrace scarves or hats in vivacious shades or bold prints that draw all eyes upward. Wear them over your sim-plest white tee or your most corporate work blazer. Lighter shades act like flaw-reducing spotlights, illuminating your face and making you look younger.

5

BOATNECK TEE
A boatneck style
makes your shoulders
look broader because
it draws focus to their
outer corners, so your
bottom half looks
skinnier by compari-
son. Also great for
you: off-the-shoulder
tops, cowl neck tops,
or wide V-necks.
Wear them over
dark-rinse, boot-cut
jeans (don't tuck them
in) and high-heeled
wedges to add extra
inches to your legs.

6

*How fabulous
is this dress?*

**ONE-SHOULDER
DRESS**
Any one-shoulder
dress will bring the
focus to the upper
part of your body and
visually "point" to the
outer edge of your
shoulders, making
your top half look
wider. Remember to
make sure the bottom
half is flared out over
your hips, not straight.

7

**TAILORED
PANTS**
Don't shy away from
pants. Embrace
mid-rise, slightly-
flared ones (not
high-waisted—they'll
make your bum look
big) in a dark solid
without side pockets,
which draw unwanted
attention to the width
of your hips. A slight
flare balances you out.

8

**SEQUIN
JACKET**
Here's what you need
to reflect the light
and draw attention
upward—remember
that anything metal-
lic or sparkly brings
the focus to wherever
you place it on your
body. (The style rule:
light and sparkly
magnifies, dark and
matte downplays.)
Throw it over your
go-to LBD or jeans
and a tee for a great
date-night look.

STYLIST RULES TO SWEAR BY

FOCUS ON PIECES THAT DRAW ATTENTION UP TO YOUR NECKLINE,

like shrugs, boleros, flutter sleeves, cap sleeves, wraps, statement necklaces, and eye-catching earrings.

DON'T WEAR ANYTHING THAT MAKES YOUR BOTTOM HALF LOOK CHUNKIER

such as side pockets, which basically draw giant arrows to the width of your body.

DON'T WEAR ANYTHING ON THE BOTTOM WITH FUSSY THINGS

like pleats, ruffles, or horizontal stripes.

DON'T WEAR FITTED PENCIL SKIRTS OR PANTS THAT ARE PATTERNED OR LIGHT-COLORED,

as they will make your bum look bigger.

DON'T WEAR FORMLESS TUNIC DRESSES THAT HIT JUST ABOVE YOUR KNEE,

since they can cling (unflatteringly) to your hips.

KEEP AWAY FROM ANKLE-STRAP SHOES.

(Unless you'd like really fat legs.)

THE BOTTOM LINE:
DRAW ATTENTION UPWARD WITH COLORS AND PRINTS, AND KEEP EVERYTHING ON YOUR BOTTOM HALF SIMPLE.

HEART PENDANT

{ BIGGER ON TOP, SMALLER ON BOTTOM }

ARE YOU SHAPED LIKE A HEART PENDANT?

☐ Do you find that shirts often struggle to contain your boobs?

☐ Do you have shapely, slender legs?

☐ Do you feel you've got broad shoulders?

☐ Do you have no defined waistline?

If you checked at least three of these questions, my darling, you're a Heart Pendant!

YOU PROBABLY HAVE A LOVE/HATE RELATIONSHIP WITH YOUR BOOBS, AM I RIGHT?

Men glance at them more often than you'd like, and I bet you've caught women raising a disapproving brow out of the corner of your eye as you saunter past. (Ignore them—they're just jealous.) You've probably got great legs, yes? But you might want to tone down your top half, so it's less of a defining feature, and create more balance by adding a little volume to the bottom. But I can almost hear you declaring in dismay: "Volume? Has she lost her mind? Won't that make me look bigger?" The answer is no. By adding a little fullness—not bulk—to your bottom half, we're going to help divert attention from a somewhat overwhelming top half, and draw all eyes to those spectacular legs for which the rest of us would kill. If you love your boobs, don't worry, we're not going to hide them. We're just going to make sure they don't totally steal the show.

HEART PENDANT SECRETS

Check out these pages throughout the book for fabulous tips on how to WOW.

117   119   121   123   125   156   162

YOUR BEST WOW FIT

WEEKEND

You've got the legs to showcase eye-catching heels or flats.

↓

A SLENDER, LONG CARDIGAN WITH A STIFFER-FABRIC SKIRT

This is one of the best looks to downplay a larger bust. A fine knit, slim-line V-neck cardigan in a solid shade (worn with a supportive bra) will downplay larger boobs, and a structured, flared skirt will draw all eyes to the lower part of your body and show off those spectacular legs.

EVENING

V-NECK DRESS WITH WIDE STRAPS, FITTED BODICE AND FULLER-FLARED HEM

The idea here is to show a hint of skin without revealing too much boobage. I know it's tempting to flaunt your cleavage at night, but showing too much can make you look heavy when you're not (trust me). Look for styles that help carve out a waist (like this fitted bodice), have wider straps (to conceal a supportive bra), and dresses with folds of fabric below the waist to balance you out and create an hourglass shape.

↑

Outrageously sexy heels call for a simple clutch.

SWIMSUIT

Sexy but supportive. Full coverage is infinitely more flattering than skimpy.

UNDERWIRE BIKINI TOP AND FULL COVERAGE BOTTOMS

The key is to look for full coverage tops with hidden structural details like underwire or built-in mesh compression liners that help to give you lift, shape, and support. Stay away from high necklines that overemphasize your bust. Go for bra-sized bikini separates that allow you to choose your cup size, and always look for wide, adjustable straps that prevent painful pinching and bouncing.

COAT

EMBELLISHED AND STREAMLINED COAT

Tailored coat styles that have embellishment or detailing around the hemline will move the focus away from your bustline. Look for coats with a covered placket (that central strip of fabric where the buttons lie) to help ensure that gaping buttons don't show.

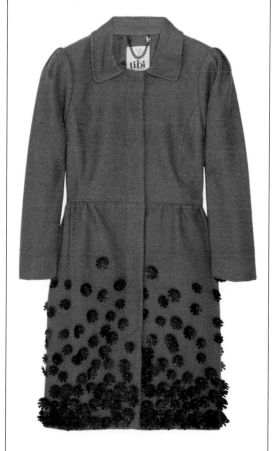

1

BUTTON-DOWN WITH STRETCH

Don't shy away from button-downs. Shirts with stretch, instead of masculine, boxy styles, will hug your curves. Look for ones with covered plackets (like the coat on the previous page) or buttons closer together to prevent any gaping. The Shirt by Rochelle Behrens or the Zarinah shirt by Carissa Rose are great options.

2

METALLIC SKIRT

Want to draw attention to your lower half and away from your top? Shine adds volume wherever you place it on the body. Pair a metallic skirt with a simple, wide-strapped tank to put the focus on your gorgeous legs.

3

V-NECK CARDIGAN

A navel-grazing V-neck minimizes your bust and elongates your torso. The secret lies in not adding any additional bulk underneath. Pair with a SkinnyShirt— a fitted tank with built-in cotton collar and cuffs (WWW.SKIN-NYSHIRT.COM). Wear with wider-leg jeans for the weekend or tailored pants for work.

4

FULL-LEG TUXEDO PANTS

A classic tuxedo pant was made for you, as its wider leg helps balance out your top half. Pair with a fitted, structured jacket to contain your bust. Avoid extreme high-waisted pants that shorten your torso and make you look top-heavy.

Obsessed!

STRAPPY, SEXY HEELS

Legs like yours beg to be shown off in heels that have just enough heft to stand up to your fuller top half. You can get away with tricky styles, like ankle-grazing shoes that showcase your slender calves.

FINE-KNIT, NON-BULKY SWEATER

Not too bulky is key, since you don't want to add weight to your upper half. V-necks help create a slender, narrow silhouette and elongate your torso. Stick to a solid shade, and pair with a printed bottom to bring attention to your lower half.

NOT YOUR TRADITIONAL BLUE JEANS

Lighter or brightly shaded jeans will show off your fabulous legs and move the focus away from your fuller bustline. Wear with a butt-skimming V-neck cardigan in a solid shade, and pair with statement heels.

KNEE-LENGTH, A-LINE SKIRT

Skirts with a soft A-line flare help to add width and balance (without bulk) to your top half. Stay away from straight, fitted skirts that highlight the difference between your upper and lower body.

STYLIST RULES TO SWEAR BY

GO FOR TOPS WITH A SLENDER V-NECK
that show a sliver of skin but draw the focus
inward and away from broader shoulders.

LOOK FOR CLOTHING THAT
HELPS LENGTHEN YOU.
It's easy to look short-waisted when you've
got large boobs, so every piece you
have should aim to s-t-r-e-t-c-h you out.

DON'T PAIR A SKINNY BOTTOM HALF
WITH A FULL TOP,
or you'll look like you're about to topple over.

LOOK FOR SHORTER JACKETS
WITH THREE BUTTONS.
They'll help hold in your boobs.

DON'T WEAR BOATNECKS OR WIDE SCOOP NECKS,
as they'll just overemphasize the broadness of your shoulders.

AND DON'T EVEN THINK ABOUT WEARING
BOLEROS, KNITS, OR SHRUGS
that draw more attention to your top half.

THE BOTTOM LINE:
USING FLARED SKIRTS, SHINE, AND COLOR, DRAW ALL EYES TOWARD YOUR FABULOUS LOWER HALF INSTEAD OF YOUR BOOBS.

COCKTAIL RING

{ A LITTLE MORE IN THE MIDDLE }

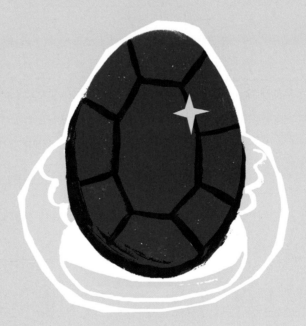

ARE YOU SHAPED LIKE A COCKTAIL RING?

☐ Do you struggle to find clothes that give you a waistline?

☐ Are you always afraid to tuck anything in?

☐ Do you get compliments on your shapely legs?

☐ Do you believe that baggier is better?

If you checked at least three of these questions, my darling, you're a Cocktail Ring!

I KNOW YOUR PHILOSOPHY, MY GORGEOUS COCKTAIL RING.

You insist on sticking to boring black because someone once said that it made you look slimmer, right? But black can be dull, dull, dull. No more, my luscious, Rubenesque darling. Let's banish the black, work on faking a waist where there isn't one, creating a longer, lean, silhouette, and carving out your dream body with the right clothes right now. I know for a fact that you most likely have a stunning décolletage (which you probably rarely show off). I know you have shapely legs (which you might be hiding under baggy, oversized pants) and you probably also have deliciously slender ankles (which I never see showcased, since they're always in frumpy-dumpy flats). So let's get you wearing some color, my cocktail ring, and I'll show you how to dress for the best you ever.

COCKTAIL RING SECRETS

Check out these pages throughout the book for fabulous tips on how to WOW.

117 119 121 123 125 156 162

WEEKEND

An eye-catching bootie adds flair to the simplest outfit. ←

RUCHED SWEATER AND WIDER-LEG PANTS

So here it's all about the art of camouflage. A brilliant wrap sweater works in a myriad of ways—you can wear it open just like you would a cardigan, but also cross-wrapped around the body to shave inches off your tummy. Wider-leg pants help extend the line of your body and create a long, lean silhouette.

EVENING

RUCHED DRESS THAT SKIMS OVER CURVES

Ruching, gathering, and artful color blocking, my darling, are your stylish best friends. Anything that is ingeniously draped across your torso will magically melt away a heavier midsection and give the illusion of a slim waistline.

↑
Keep your dress fabric matte, and add the dazzle with a sparkling clutch and heels.
↓

SWIMSUIT

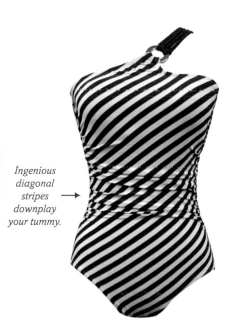

Ingenious diagonal stripes → *downplay your tummy.*

SEXY STRIPED ONE-PIECE

The key is to raise the bustline to stretch out your torso, and camouflage your tum with strategically placed ruching, shirring, or diagonal chevron stripes. Look for waist-minimizing fabrics like stretchy spandex that hold you in. If you want to try a bikini, look for high-rise bottoms that hit just below the navel for their tummy-toning effect. Strapless or asymmetrical tops will bring the focus up toward sexy shoulders and décolletage.

COAT

DARING ANIMAL-PRINT TRENCH

Don't shy away from anything belted. Instead, create a shapelier middle by going for a classic belted trench: its narrow, bulk-free silhouette and belt create the illusion of a trimmer waistline. And forget boring black; embrace bolder prints instead.

WARDROBE ESSENTIALS

1

WHITE WRAP SHIRT

The crisscross effect tricks the eye into seeing a more defined waist, and the wrapped fabric cleverly fakes curves if you tie the knot at the side. Wear one under a jacket with pants or a slightly A-line skirt for work, or alone with jeans on the weekend. Add a long necklace to create an even leaner look.

2

LONGER-LENGTH RUCHED TOP

Look for tops with clever draping or ruching that skims down the side of your torso. Pair with jeans (hemmed to the ground so your legs look even longer) and high heels. Add a skinny cardigan or jacket if it's cold outside.

3

V-NECK COCKTAIL DRESS WITH WIDE STRAPS

Ultra-deep V-necks elongate your neckline and point to the center slither of your frame (deflecting attention away from your sides); wide straps allow for a supportive bra underneath.

4

FITTED, NARROW-LAPEL BLAZER

Get rid of anything double-breasted and go for a form-fitting, narrow-lapel blazer that nips in at your torso. Wear it unbuttoned over a colored or printed shirt to create the appearance of a trimmer waistline.

5

BELTED SHEATH DRESS

A belted dress helps create a waistline (where there isn't one) and makes your entire body look leaner. Pair with a long-sleeve, slim-fitting cardigan in a vivid shade if you want to cover your arms.

6

DARK-WASH JEANS WITH STRETCH

A darker wash automatically slims your legs down and the stretch will have some "give" to it so that the jeans conform to your body. Go for a wider-leg silhouette—too-slim jeans hug all the wrong places.

7

A SLIM-FIT KNIT WITH EMBELLISH-MENT

A dressy cardigan is a super simple solution to downplay a thicker torso. Look for deep Vs to slice up a wide midsection, and embellishment details placed toward the center panel. Slip a tailored button-down underneath to wear it for the office, or pair with dark-wash jeans and heels for a night out.

8

These are just darling!

EYE-CATCHING BALLET FLATS

Embellished or brightly colored flats add a splash of interest to your weekend jeans and tees. Plus, they bring attention to slim ankles. (I guarantee you have slim ankles.)

STYLIST RULES TO SWEAR BY

A TAILORED, WIDER-LEG PANT WILL LOOK SENSATIONAL

because it creates one long, slender line.
And side seams that are angled slightly toward
the front of your leg will help create a leaner look.

WEAR CHUNKIER-HEELED SHOES;

delicate kitten heels can make you look like an elephant
in heels. (My full-figured friend once told me that,
and we laughed so hard I nearly wet myself.)

USE COLOR BLOCKING TO YOUR ADVANTAGE.

Anything that's lighter in the middle than
it is at the sides will draw the eyes toward the center
of your body and make you look thinner.

DON'T WEAR SHORT, BOXY JACKETS

that make you look…like a short box.

DON'T WEAR THIN, FLIMSY FABRICS

that cling to and overemphasize every bulge and bump.

BUT DO STOCK UP ON TAILORED JACKETS

that help carve out a waistline.

THE BOTTOM LINE:
DON'T TRY TO COVER UP YOUR LACK OF A WAIST; JUST MASTER THE ILLUSION OF CREATING A SLIMMER, TRIMMER ONE.

LIPSTICK

{ FAIRLY STRAIGHT UP AND DOWN }

ARE YOU SHAPED LIKE A LIPSTICK?

☐	☐	☐	☐
Do you feel you look too "boyish"?	Do you have no defined waistline?	Do you want to add womanly curves?	Do you need to boost your bust?

If you checked at least three of these questions, my darling, you're a Lipstick!

SO YOU'D LIKE TO HAVE A FEW MORE CURVES AND JUST A LITTLE MORE, WELL...SHAPE?

The irony is that all your friends probably drone on about how lucky you are that you can wear absolutely anything, right? "Oh, you can't have any problems," they declare scornfully. "I mean, you're tall and slim—anything will fit." But we both know differently. Baggy clothes look completely shapeless on you, right? And you often struggle to find things that give you any sort of feminine shape. You can easily veer off into pre-pubescent boy or clothing hanger territory with your straight up-and-down figure, and you're envious of those with killer curves. Don't worry, my slender sweetheart. What we're going to do is ramp up your WOW and dazzle everyone in your orbit by creating curves that would give J.Lo herself a run for her money.

LIPSTICK SECRETS

Check out these pages throughout the book for fabulous tips on how to WOW.

| 117 | 119 | 121 | 123 | 125 | 156 | 162 |

YOUR BEST WOW FIT

WEEKEND

Stripes give the illusion of a shape; chunky boots add heft.

HORIZONTAL-STRIPED SWEATER AND LIGHTER-WASH JEANS WITH POCKETS

The key is in the bold, horizontal stripes that add welcome width to straight shapes. (They lead the eye across instead of up and down.) And pants in a lighter wash help amplify, too; look for jeans with defined, embellished back pockets that create the look of a fuller butt.

EVENING

A DRESS WITH SHEEN

If you have a straighter figure you can pull off a sparkly little number in a wildly glamorous fabric without looking like you're off to Vegas. The great thing about metallics is that they help reflect the light (creating Kardashian-like curves), and all that shimmer and shine will give your slender body far more dimension. Find something with ruffles or layers and you'll create the illusion of more va-voom than you know what to do with.

A dress like this just needs a simple evening clutch and sandals without frills and ruffles.

SWIMSUIT

↑

*Super cute ruffles and
embellishment details
add extra volume.*

↓

FLIRTY PUSH-UP BIKINI

Padded, corset like push-ups and details like
ruffles and bows work wonders to create a
curvaceous shape. Go for prints with curves
of their own to give more volume to your
bustline. Adjustable necklines or straps let you
produce a more dramatic push-up effect. But
you can also go sporty—color-blocked one-
pieces that divide the body with bold panels
of color is another way to add shape.

COAT

RUFFLED AND STRIPED COAT

Any extra detailing on the fabric, ruffles, or
exaggerated seaming will add more dimension.
Look for belted coats that help carve out a
defined waistline, or go for embellishments
like pleating around the booty. Double-
breasted panels and wide stripes add even
more welcome shape.

WARDROBE ESSENTIALS

A DRESS THAT LOOKS LIKE SEPARATES

Break up the straight line of a lean frame with different shades on your top and bottom. Anything with pockets on the bust gives the appearance of bigger boobs. Go for belted pieces to help create a waist, even if you're straight as a board.

KITTEN HEELS

The magic of kitten heels for this shape is that they make no-shape legs look beyond curvaceous. The secret? The daintier the heel, the curvier your calves will look by comparison.

STRETCH DENIM JACKET

The stretch conforms to your frame and makes you look curvier; pockets and studs will add welcome volume. But don't pair denim with denim (I don't care what the trend du jour is, it's hard to pull off). Instead, wear over a flirty, floaty summer dress or pair with a horizontal-striped tee and cargo pants.

PRINTED, TEXTURED PENCIL SKIRT

Don't drown your slender frame in anything baggy; opt for a bold print and texture that will add shape to your figure. Pair a skirt like this with a solid, fitted button-down shirt, pumps, and a skinny belt for work, or a V-neck cardigan and flat boots for the weekend.

*These
are just
fabulous!*

CHUNKY TURTLENECK

Yup, turtlenecks were made for small busts (unlike your larger-busted sisters who can look "all boob" and as if they're about to fall over in turtlenecks). Pair with flared jeans on the weekend, or wear one to work tucked into tailored pants (cinched with a sen-sational belt) to carve out a waistline.

KNEE-HIGH RIDING BOOTS

If you've got super slender legs go for flat, equestrian-style boots that you can slip easily over skinny jeans. Add a long, fine-knit sweater that you can wear belted, and you've got a no-thought-required weekend look.

TEXTURED OR PLEATED SKIRT

For evening, look for skirts with some kind of ruffle, pleating, or shirring that lends volume without bulk. The trick is to keep the rest of the look relatively simple—there's a lot going on with a skirt like this—so just add a simple fitted tank or a long-sleeve tee and heels.

ONE-SHOULDER TOP

Necklines like halters or one-shoulder styles give the illusion of dimension and a curvier silhouette. Add statement earrings for even more interest above the shoulder line. Anything with a high neck or cutaway sleeves will also show off your slender arms.

STYLIST RULES TO SWEAR BY

WEAR BOLDER NECKLACES
that visually point to your chest
and make you look bustier.

STRONG BLOCKS OF COLOR
WORK BRILLIANTLY FOR YOU;
they add welcome width to a slender frame and
help create shape for your narrow silhouette.

PANTS OR JACKETS WITH CURVE-BUILDING
FLAP POCKETS OR PEPLUMS
(that no other shape can pull off!)
were made for you.

EMBRACE BELTED PIECES AND STIFFER FABRICS
that create the illusion of shapeliness.

DON'T WEAR BAGGY, OVERSIZED CLOTHES
that camouflage any curves you do have.

AND DON'T EVEN THINK ABOUT WEARING
LOW-RISE, BOYISH PANTS
that make you look, well…like a boy.

THE BOTTOM LINE:
YOU CAN PULL OFF THE EMBELLISHMENTS, VOLUME, AND PRINTS THAT YOUR CURVIER SISTERS CAN'T— SO HAVE FUN CREATING SOME SHAPE.

BODY SHAPES THROUGHOUT HISTORY

Time to get a little perspective. I've created this totally non-scientific timeline to show you darlings that there is no such thing as an *ideal* body shape. All shapes are gorgeous. See for yourself.

A REALLY LONG TIME AGO

Eve asks Adam if these leaves make her bum look big. He thinks she looks hot, but he is not sure how to answer. She's a COCKTAIL RING.

1400s

Boticelli paints *The Birth of Venus*. She's definitely a FRAGRANCE BOTTLE.

1800s

During the Victorian era, the ideal body type for women is plump, fleshy, and curvaceous. Here we see our first glimpse of SUNGLASSES in the form of corsets that make teeny-weeny waists. Are corsets fashionable? Yes. Comfortable? I don't think so.

1920s

The dawn of the flapper era makes everyone desperate to be a LIPSTICK. Those who aren't lucky enough to have this figure strap down their boobs to fake the flat-as-a-pancake profile essential for those straight sheath dresses.

1950s

Our SUNGLASSES girl is back—with a pointy bra, tiny waist and full bum. (Though don't forget that Marilyn was a size 12.)

1960s

The pendulum swings back to **LIPSTICK.** Twiggy becomes an instant icon, with her stream-lined sex appeal. She is also 91 pounds and has a body type nearly impossible to achieve for most grown women.

1970s

The poster of Farrah Fawcett in her iconic red bathing suit sells 12 million copies and accentuates her curves to make her look like SUNGLASSES. Swimwear with strategic cutouts are all the rage.

1980s

While toned and athletic-looking is all the rage with muscles, spandex, and Jane Fonda, **LIPSTICKS** still pervade the runway and feed into body issues and anorexia.

1990s

Ah...big boobs, yet slimmer every-where else? Think Pamela Anderson in that red *Baywatch* bathing suit and plastic surgery. A definite HEART PENDANT.

TODAY & THE FUTURE

Women will finally realize that **COCKTAIL RINGS,** FRAGRANCE BOTTLES, **LIPSTICKS,** SUNGLASSES, and HEART PENDANTS all have their chal-lenges. They will love their bodies for what they are.

PETITE

{ 5'3" OR UNDER }

Now that you know what body shape you are, you might be asking, "But what are the insider tricks to dressing if I'm short?" Keeping your body shape in mind, here are a few key tips to help you make the most out of your petite stature.

WARDROBE ESSENTIALS

SLIM KNIT CARDIGAN

Go for snug-fitting skinny knits instead of bulky, slouchy ones. The idea is to find pieces that won't overwhelm your frame and make you look shorter.

TAILORED JACKET

Embrace tailored jackets that hit at or above the hip, and keep away from anything boxy or square.

DARK-WASH JEANS

Go for a dark, uniform wash that makes legs look longer. Keep jeans hemmed to the ground to heighten the lengthening effect. (No crops. Ever.)

SMALL PRINTS

Embrace head-to-toe prints, but make sure that the repeating print is no bigger than the palm of your hand. (You don't want to look like you're wearing a tablecloth.)

WEAR SHEER OR LIGHT HOSIERY
to help make legs look longer.

CHECK OUT THE JUNIOR SECTION,
where you'll often find brilliant buys for your height.

LOOK FOR LINES SPECIFICALLY TAILORED FOR PETITES,
as details like pocket placement, sleeve length,
and a higher knee break are factored in.

NEVER WEAR CAPRIS
unless you want to look short and dumpy.

DON'T WEAR HEELS THAT ARE TOO HIGH,
as you can easily veer into the "raiding the dress-up box" category.

AND DON'T EVEN THINK ABOUT WEARING SKIRTS THAT HIT MIDCALF.
They're the quickest route to Frumpy Dumpy-dom.

TALL

{ OVER 5'10" }

Okay, so what if you're tall? Still focus on your specific body shape,
and learn these insider style tricks to help you
make the most of your fabulous Amazonian stature.

WARDROBE ESSENTIALS

COLOR-BLOCKED DRESS

Add dimension to a long torso with color blocking. A bright top and different-colored bottom create visual interest.

CHUNKY WIDE BELT

An oversized belt will carve out your waistline and divide your body into two shorter halves.

HIGH HEELS

Embrace your height proudly. Wear heels and don't apologize for every great inch you were born with.

MIXED-FABRIC COAT

Look for coats broken into distinct sections to add more differentiation to your frame (and keep you from looking like one long beanpole).

GO FOR HIGH-WAIST PANTS AND FULLER TOPS
that create two distinct sections on your body.

WEAR STRUCTURED SEPARATES
that create a more shapely stature.

SHOP BRANDS THAT MAKE PANTS IN EXTRA-LONG LENGTHS,
and layer lightweight long-sleeve tees under jackets.
Push up the sleeves and create contrasts
with different prints, textures, and fabrics.

NEVER WEAR ANYTHING THAT'S SHRUNKEN
or it will look like the washing machine
did it by mistake.

DON'T CHOOSE SUPER SHORT MINIS
for the same reason as above.

AND DON'T EVEN THINK ABOUT WEARING VERTICAL STRIPES,
which will stretch you out even more;
choose plaid or horizontal stripes instead.

THE 3 MOST IMPORTANT RULES TO FOLLOW

①

EMBRACE AND
LOVE THE SHAPE
YOU HAVE.

②

ONLY WEAR CLOTHES THAT
FLATTER YOUR FIGURE.

③

IGNORE WHAT YOUR FRIENDS
AND CELEBRITIES ARE
WEARING BECAUSE THEIR
BODY SHAPES ARE
COMPLETELY DIFFERENT
FROM YOURS.

(repeat daily)

CONFESSIONS
FROM THE CONFIDENTIAL FASHION FILES

Okay, even though I was destined to become a fashionista, I made some gargantuan fashion mistakes before I figured out what really flattered my shape. Of course, with age comes wisdom—and everyone's entitled to their fair share of heinous fashion mistakes while they're young and foolish. Although I've never been a Skinny Minnie, I've never wished my body to be anything other than what it is. I'm a classic Fragrance Bottle and I don't waste time coveting styles or cuts that don't work for me. I've got a slender upper half, a relatively small waist and big ol' hips, bum, and thighs. My bottom is my "problem" area, but everything in my wardrobe works to make me look taller and skinnier than I actually am. I don't wear spindly little heels that make my chunky legs look chunkier. If I'm wearing a shorter-length skirt during fall, I'll pair it with dark, opaque hosiery and knee-high boots so people think I have supermodel-worthy legs. (Spoiler: I don't. Ha! You should see me naked!)

So when I consult with my clients, I scratch my head at those who insist on going for something that is so obviously wrong for their body shape. "How can you love clothes that don't love you back?" I ask, puzzled, as they're about to pluck a shrunken, bum-grazing cardi off the rack that I know will barely contain their giant boobs.

So, my darlings, figure out your body shape and make that form the basis for *everything you wear from now on*. If there's only one thing you take away from this chapter, it's this: Forget your size—and embrace your *shape*.

HOW TO WOW

LEARN WHAT REALLY GOES ON BEHIND THE FASHION SCENES

So many of us are baffled and overwhelmed by exactly what clothes to wear and what makeup to put on. You see, the industry is desperate to sell us stuff we don't really need. I'm going to blow the lid off and share the insider secrets that really work to give you that WOW FACTOR. I'll share the honest truth about the tricks we use to seduce you and give you advice that genuinely garners results.

I'll show you how to look your best with proven insider knowledge about how to turn your dream self into your real self.

You see, I've been a fashion and beauty editor a long time, and I've got insider stuff to spill. I've been front and center at runway shows around the globe—London, Paris, Hong Kong, and New York—and have watched model after model saunter down a gazillion catwalks. I've written for major glossies like *Vogue*, *Marie Claire*, *Cosmopolitan*, *Lucky*, and *Shape*, and styled hundreds of real women on TV shows you probably watch every day. So let's get started with what really goes on in the fashion and beauty world…

…AND THE INSIDER TRUTH ABOUT COVER SHOOTS, MAKEOVERS, AND EVERYONE TRYING TO SELL YOU STUFF.

WHAT THE MAGAZINES SAY

"Celeb X strolled onto the set bubbly and early! Fresh from a relaxing jaunt to Paris with her movie star beau, she slipped seamlessly into every item of clothing she tried and then tucked into a hearty meal!"

WHAT REALLY HAPPENS

First of all, celebs rarely slip into anything seamlessly. Many have insanely fragile egos and ludicrous demands about what they absolutely will, or won't, be photographed in. Like the A-list superstar who insisted she'd only agree to be shot if her arms were completely covered (a challenge because we needed her in a bikini). But after endless, tortuous late-night discussions with the star's diva-like stylist, we'll do our "fittings" and attempt to wiggle the star into a few pieces. A particularly evil strategy I like is to hold up an item and gush ego-flattering compliments: "Now, I know this is a size double zero, but it's going to be huge on you…" is what I generally say and it makes them open to trying on anything. And since I've already cut out every size tag (God forbid she has to wear a size four instead of a zero) the star is none the wiser. You see, celebs are just as pointlessly obsessed with size as everyone else.

WHAT YOU CAN ACTUALLY DO

From now on, I want you to ignore the number on the label. I only want you to focus on how it fits. (I can see you rolling your eyes, and I know you don't want to read this.) The fact is that no one knows what size you're actually wearing. What other people do notice, however, is if you're squeezed into something obviously too snug, like that muffin top spilling out over your too-tight jeans. Don't get hung up on the wrong size just because you can't bear the thought of going up one. And don't be fooled: The fashion industry has figured out every one of your insecurities, and plays to them with the devious art of "vanity sizing." This is where they'll label something in a smaller size to cater to your size obsession. Ever noticed that in some stores you're an 8, but in others you can fit easily into a 4? Which store do you think you're more likely to shop in? Buyer beware: this is just an industry trick to seduce you.

INSIDE SCOOP

Behind that perfectly draped gown on the model is an army of safety pins and bulldog clips to make everything look immaculate.

WHAT THE MAGAZINES SAY

"Celeb X arrived at the set barefaced. We simply dabbed on a hint of blush and a swipe of cherry pink gloss. Buy these products that we used, and you too can get the look— in less than five minutes!"

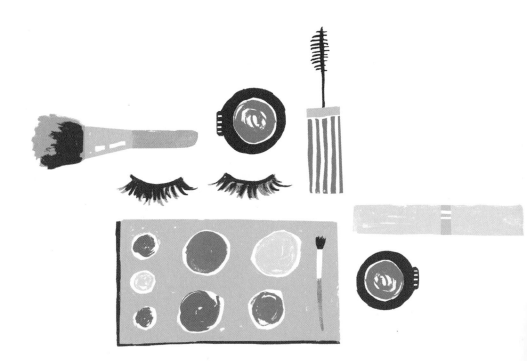

WHAT REALLY HAPPENS

Here's the truth behind those magazine cover credits: usually the makeup we insist the model is wearing is not that at all. More often than not, what we claim to be the products used to create her look are the cosmetic brands that are spending the most on advertising with us that month. And while we may have used a similar shade on our starlet, the makeup artist will have blended it with at least five other colors to create that particular concoction.

You see, most makeup artists carry around tiny paint palettes filled with a variety of colors to create custom shades. It's often an arsenal of various shades and brands that they'll blend together to make a special color for that particular celebrity. And the process, by the way, takes hours and hours and hours (not minutes).

INSIDE SCOOP

Fake a dewy, moisturized face with makeup artists' secret weapon: Benefit High Beam. Apply to cheeks, brow bone, and even in the Cupid's bow of your lip, and dab on your chin. Even the driest skin looks like it's lit from within.

WHAT YOU CAN ACTUALLY DO

Don't be fooled into buying the exact makeup you're told is on the cover model. Apart from the fact that the shade probably doesn't exist, the color on your skin tone might look completely different. If you've fallen in love with a particular glossy red lip for example, you should note that bluish reds can be tricky on olive or tan complexions and generally look best if you have fair skin. Orangey reds flatter olive complexions and pinkish reds look fabulous if you're dark-skinned.

Now, when it comes to prepping the skin, most makeup artists tend to follow a basic routine: they'll start with a hydrating moisturizer that soaks in easily (I love Orlane's Super-Moisturizing Light Cream), then blend a natural-looking foundation or tinted moisturizer that matches the skin tone exactly (Clinique's RepairWear Laser Focus All-Smooth Makeup SPF 15 is a celeb makeup artist fave: it's lightweight, gives picture-perfect dewy coverage, and comes in a dozen shades). Later, I'll share more time-tested insider tricks to make you a cover model.

WHAT THE MAGAZINES SAY
"Get these effortless waves by using just a quick spray of this fabulous new product!"

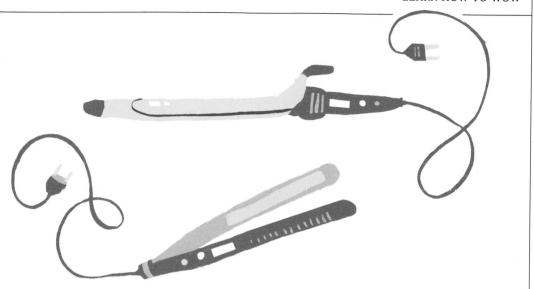

WHAT REALLY HAPPENS

Ha! Trust me, there's absolutely nothing effortless about that hair—moreover, it's got nothing to do with product. For covers, hairstylists often use wigs, falls, or clip-in custom-made extensions. So if there are certain stars you'd swear have mountains of generously lustrous curls, I can tell you that they most likely have just a few baby-fine wisps. Even those who do have naturally thick hair benefit from additional extensions. Particularly if there's a wind machine on the set. (Without fake hair, the celeb can easily morph into a tornado-ravaged wreck.)

WHAT YOU CAN ACTUALLY DO

Few of us have those effortless waves naturally, so try this secret to create a cover-worthy look at home: spritz a volumizing spray at the roots, turn head upside down and blow-dry. (Phytovolume Actif from Phyto actually thickens the diameter of each strand.) Then dig out those old Velcro rollers your mother swore by. Brush 3-inch-wide sections of hair upward, place the roller at the back of the hair section, and roll downward toward the scalp. Flash blow-dry on a high heat and mist with a light hairspray (L'Oreal's Elnett is what on-set stylists can't live without because it brushes out so easily) then unroll and run fingers though the strands.

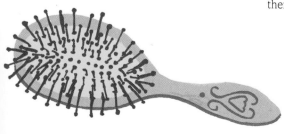

WHAT THE MAGAZINES SAY

"Celeb X loves to eat, but she keeps her body in shape by doing yoga and Pilates!"

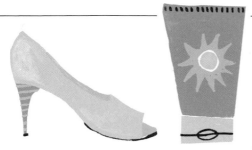 

WHAT REALLY HAPPENS

Hmmm. Celebs love to give quotes about their envious bodies and how they're just lucky. I can tell you that celebs work zealously for those biceps and resort to ludicrous extremes to be ready for their close-up. On shoot days, many eat practically nothing and enjoy a hearty lunch of a lettuce leaf and a sip of Pellegrino. One star even ate ice chips instead of drinking water in case her tummy looked bloated.

Another trick that they rely on to get sculpted-looking abs on cover shoots? Self-tanner. Some show up with their own spray-tan artists in tow to create that ultra-ripped torso. And we shoot them in heels to lengthen their legs and make their butts stick out to perfection. (One star even insisted on wearing heels in the swimming pool.) Lastly, once the shot has been taken, it goes into numerous editing rounds, where we might even cut and paste the star's head onto different shots of her body.

WHAT YOU CAN ACTUALLY DO

Oh, how I wish I had the magic solution. The hard truth is…get yourself into a regular exercise routine and eat less. (Sorry.) If you're pressed for time, for toned arms do twenty minutes of arm circles and free-weight lifts each morning. Push-ups are possibly one of the most effective exercises and don't require an expensive gym membership. Schedule at least 30 minutes of weight lifting or cardio into your daily routine and make exercise as non-negotiable as brushing your teeth.

Here's a look-skinnier insider secret from the set: rub a light-reflecting body lotion over your upper arms to make them look slimmer. I'm obsessed with Michael Kors's deliriously scented, whipped Glimmer Body Creme, which leaves a glamorous golden glow. Or fake slimmer-looking legs by rubbing a gleaming body lotion down just the center of your shins. Sally Hansen's Airbrush Legs is a good one that's water-resistant and helps cover veins and imperfections.

INSIDE SCOOP

A secret from the set: always apply self-tanner to lotion-free skin (as moisturizer makes it streaky), and cover cuticles and palms with Vaseline to avoid telltale signs that your glow came from a bottle.

WHAT THE MAGAZINES SAY
"Floral!
Nautical!
Tribal!"

WHAT REALLY HAPPENS

Style pages often feature a collection of "favorite things" from editors. But editors don't know what will actually work in your wardrobe. What we do is sit around in meetings and come up with a theme, like "floral," for example. Then we'll call a public relations company that represents fashion brands, and find out what they've got that might work with our "floral" page. We'll browse through lookbooks and linesheets, honing in on anything featuring that particular trend.

But these are not necessarily wearable pieces. They simply speak to the medium of the magazine's double-page spread. Pieces are chosen based on how they look on the page, or if we're BFFs with the PR girls. The spread is purely inspirational; fabulous if you're rifling mindlessly through a mag while sitting under the dryer at the hair salon, but often completely useless if you're trying to figure out what to wear in real life.

WHAT YOU CAN ACTUALLY DO

Be your own fashion editor. Before you dash out to snatch up everything that looks pretty on the page, start thinking about whether it really works with your current wardrobe. I'd like you to think in entire outfits, not specific pieces that don't work with anything in your closet.

Create your own Editor's Pick pages by rifling through your own photos, and earmarking the ones in which you're wearing something that makes you feel incredible. Can you evoke the same aesthetic into your wardrobe every day? Look at patterns and colors that flatter you, the home décor that makes you feel relaxed, the accessories that make you sparkle, and even movies that inspire. All these elements help create a look that is uniquely *you*. Once you step back and take a good hard look at the images you've culled, you can better articulate your own sense of style.

Incorporate whatever you're drawn to in fashion spreads by adding just a dash of it. While not everyone can afford that $5,000 tangerine tunic featured in a magazine, every woman can introduce touches of color into her wardrobe in the form of an accessory: a bag, a shoe, a scarf.

TV & MAGAZINE MAKEOVERS

WHAT THE MAGAZINES SAY

"Steph hasn't had a haircut in decades, and needs a complete overhaul."

WHAT REALLY HAPPENS

It's true that the more dramatic the result, the better the segment. The problem occurs when the poor makeover subject gets home and doesn't have a clue how to re-create her new look. When it comes to clothing for TV make-overs, we work hard to shape and minimize, and create the illusion of a great body so you, the viewer, can see the impact immediately.

I often have barely more than an hour to complete my transformation because my subjects usually have busy, real lives that don't involve spending an eternity trying on dozens of outfits. So it's my job to come up with head-to-toe looks that work perfectly. Many times I won't even have ever met my subjects in person. I'll simply analyze their photo to determine their body shape, and shop for their ideal outfit from that picture.

So here's my insider secret: I'll hone in on the precise style that works for the woman's body type. I won't waste time browsing racks of flimsy blouses if she's full-busted and might need more of a structured top to look great. I won't pick out a skinny pencil skirt if my makeover subject has a large butt and heavy thighs, as she'll look like Ten Ton Tessie on TV. If she's straight up and down, I'll only choose pieces that I know won't make her look like a beanpole. If she's curvy I know that I need to find silhouettes that make her longer and leaner. And I'll pick out everything in a number of sizes and always add at least two to the one she gives me.

WHAT YOU CAN ACTUALLY DO

Recognize if you're in a rut. We choose our subjects for TV because they've had the same look since they were teens, and we know we'll be able to make a huge difference. But just because you don't look like you stepped out of the 1970s, you're not exempt. I'll bet there are at least three elements of your look that you can update.

Vow to make at least three small tweaks to your style each season (things like a brightly colored scarf, a new shade of eye shadow, or something as obvious as a fresh trim) to make sure you're on a rut-free course. (If you don't, you'd be surprised how quickly a decade slips away and suddenly you're featured on the *Today Show*'s time-warp segment.) Try on the pieces in your closet you haven't worn in a while and take a good hard look at whether they really work. Is that skirt pulling across your hips and drawing attention to the width of your butt? Is that top with the epaulettes accentuating your linebacker shoulders? (Probably not your best look.) When you're next out shopping, remember to work with your body shape and save yourself a fortune by getting it right—like a professional fashion editor—within minutes.

PRIVATE STYLING

"A personal stylist is a luxury reserved only for celebrities and the wealthy."

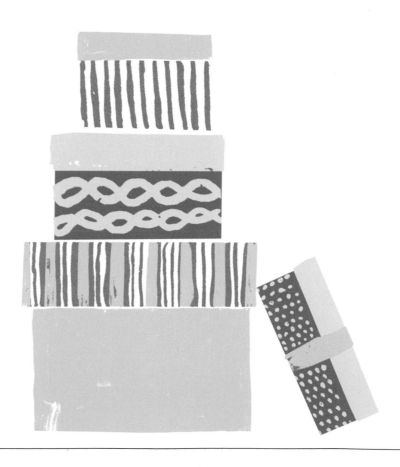

WHAT REALLY HAPPENS

Anyone with even the smallest budget can benefit from the help of a private stylist. First, learn the difference between personal shoppers and private stylists. Personal shoppers work for a store, and have an extensive working knowledge of the merchandise for which they earn commission. And while there are definite advantages to personal shoppers who know the stores' products well, they also earn their living by how much you buy. A personal shopper won't know about your lifestyle or the holes in your wardrobe. She may not realize that you're about to purchase your thirty-fifth pair of jeans, and that what you really need are pants to wear to work. So make a list of what you need to buy and stick to it. (A goof-proof way to detect a personal shopper's motives: if you're trying on sparkly cocktail frocks and share that you never go anywhere more glam than the playground, gauge her reaction. If she replies cheerily, "But I'm sure you'll find an occasion," she may not have your best interests at heart.)

Private stylists, on the other hand, are not beholden to one brand or designer. Think of personal stylists like a personal trainer for your wardrobe—a good one will motivate and inspire you to look sensational all on your own. So the first thing I do is examine a client's current wardrobe (in all its natural, gloriously chaotic state) to establish a strategy. I'm a big believer that a few tweaks may be all that's needed.

I'll have a chat with my clients about their lifestyles, so I can get to the heart of the problem: maybe it's a new phase in life (transitioning from mummy back to mogul) or maybe she needs an updated fall or summer wardrobe, or has lost (or gained) weight and needs some fresher pieces. Is she always in a rush to get ready? Or does she enjoy a leisurely morning with time to spare? Where does she spend most of her time? In the playground, or hashing out deals in the boardroom? Then we get to work on analyzing and reorganizing her closet in a practical and easy way. If there are any missing items, we hit the stores. My clients who have no time to shop often prefer me to do it for them, and I deliver edited pieces to their home that they can browse at leisure.

When we've settled on the purchases, I'll create head-to-toe looks that I'll style exactly as she might wear them—rolling up the sleeves, layering with a necklace or a scarf, or turning up the collar. And lastly, I'll snap photos so she knows how to style it all together herself.

PRIVATE STYLING

WHAT YOU CAN ACTUALLY DO

Be your own ruthless stylist. Take a step back from your closet and view it through the eyes of a professional. Forget that your hubby loves certain outfits (definitely keep them on hand, but you might move them to one side for this exercise). The same goes for those sentimental pieces from a decade ago. Some things just need to be organized better so you can identify what you have that still works and figure out what you might need to replace.

Maybe the addition of the ideal pair of pants is the solution you need to wear all those great tops you have? One of the most common phrases I hear is, "I don't know what goes with this…" which is why I guide my clients to buy head-to-toe looks, rather than splurging on impulsive, separate pieces that exist only in a vacuum.

Before you head to the store, create a game plan to maximize your valuable time. Learn the layout of the store to which you're going, have a laundry list of things you need, and head directly for the brands and designers that you know work best for your shape.

INSIDE SCOOP

With private clients, I can always tell if they're hanging on to a certain item they shouldn't be. Maybe it fit a decade ago, but sadly they'll never get it past their ankles again. Giving it away opens up an unbelievable expanse to embrace a gorgeous new you as you are today. (See? Years of expensive therapy sorted out.)

STYLE QUESTIONS
TO ASK YOURSELF AS YOUR OWN STYLIST

HAVE I GOT TWENTY OF THESE?
Chances are you don't need ten red T-shirts. Keep half and toss
(or donate to a friend) the ones that don't make the cut.

DID IT COST ME A FORTUNE,
SO I CAN'T BEAR TO THROW IT AWAY?
What's pricier is the valuable prime real estate that it's taking
up in your closet. Reclaim your premium wardrobe space.

DOES IT FIT?
A wildly obvious one, but those skinny jeans you're
hoping to fit into are collecting dust. By the time they fit over
your thighs the skinny trend will be long gone.

DOES THIS ITEM WORK IN MY REAL LIFE?
If you bought a divine sundress thinking you'd be
wearing it to a garden party and you're still waiting for the
invitation, it's time to let it go.

IS THIS WHO I WANT TO BE?
If it's the epitome of your style philosophy, keep it.
If it's ripped, faded, or looks like it's seen better days, step away.

WOULD I LIKE IT IF...?
If it would be fabulous shorter, with a set of new
buttons, or without the ruffled sleeves, keep it and take
it to the tailor to be tweaked. Today.

TOP 5 LIES
THE FASHION INDUSTRY TELLS YOU

CELEBS LOOK EFFORTLESS BECAUSE THEY PUT IN NO EFFORT.

Not true. There's a major, hardworking entourage
behind the scenes that make it all look "effortless."

YOU CAN TRUST A SALESPERSON AT THE STORE TO TELL YOU IF SOMETHING DOESN'T FLATTER YOU.

Nope. They're earning a big fat commission
on those $400 pants that make you look big and fat.

FASHION = EXPENSIVE.

Lies. You can make anything inexpensive look stylish.
It's all about how you wear it.

MAKEOVERS ARE FOR PEOPLE WHO NEED MAJOR HELP.

We might select makeover candidates who yield
results for an impressive TV impact, but mini-makeovers
are ideal for those who want to freshen up their look.

YOU MUST BUY IT SINCE IT'S ADVERTISED IN ALL THE TOP MAGAZINES.

Don't be fooled by expensive ad campaigns.

CONFESSIONS
FROM THE CONFIDENTIAL
FASHION FILES

Live TV can be fraught; like one of my near-disastrous spray-tanning segments. The idea was that the TV host would pluck an audience member to be "tanned" in front of a live audience. But since we all knew how a startled novice could emerge with brown streaks and orange fingernails, we'd perform the "tanning" during the set break instead. With clever editing, our girl would emerge with a deep, sun-drenched golden glow within a matter of minutes.

So on cue, the host asked the audience for "volunteers". But then picked out the wrong girl instead of our preselected audience member. Slightly alarmed, I led the milky-white young lady toward the tanning booth. "Don't worry," I whispered. "We won't really turn it on."

We were just about to cut to commercial, when there was a loud hissing in my earpiece. "Turn on the machine!" demanded the producer as a cameraman leaned over my right shoulder, pointing his lens into the booth as my Casper-like subject blinked at me, owl-like. Within seconds my lily-white makeover subject was doused in jets of dark tanning spray from all directions, her arms flailing wildly.

"Cut!" yelled the producer, as we went to commercial. I flung open the booth to find my horrified model drenched in thick chocolate streaks dripping down her cheeks, arms and legs. "Does anyone have a towel?" I whimpered. No one replied; too busy changing set furniture.

"So let's see our golden girl!" said the host brightly.

I led my zebra-striped victim toward the host, surreptitiously scrubbing her arms with a stack of hastily grabbed paper towels, and braced myself for the awkward silence of the audience. Luckily, a quick-thinking cameraman spotted the disastrous mess and quickly pulled away instead of zooming in, as the taken-aback TV host hurriedly segued to the next segment.

3

FULL-COVERAGE REPORT

FIND WHAT YOU NEED FOR YOUR BOOBS AND YOUR BUM

An entire chapter on bras and knickers? Yawn. The problem, though, is that 80 percent of you are wearing the wrong size bra. So that's why I'm devoting this chapter to the secrets we fashion editors employ for what to wear underneath. You see, you're wasting precious, hard-earned cash on designer duds if you pair them with the wrong undergarments. And you already know that for every celeb on the red carpet, there's an arsenal of high-tech control artillery underneath, right? The key is to gather a wardrobe of bras, panties, and shape-wear that allows you to wear absolutely everything you own and buy anything you want.

What you'll learn from this chapter is that for whatever you wear from now on—whether it's got a deep-plunging neckline or it's super sheer or fits snugly across your tummy—there is the ideal undergarment to create your WOW FACTOR and make your look appear effortless.

Let's lift up your boobs so you look longer and leaner, smooth out those less-than-welcome lumps and bumps so everything drapes exquisitely, and use underwear to look skinnier (or shapelier) in minutes. Yup, I'm going undercover to give you the full scoop…

…AND HOW TO GET THE BRAS AND PANTIES THAT SUCK YOU IN, PUSH YOU UP, AND PUT IT ALL IN THE RIGHT PLACE.

HOW TO
SHOP FOR A BRA

Your first step to establish the right fit is to get professionally fitted (it's a free service) by either heading to a large department store (ask for the lead specialist who's been there the longest) or a specialty lingerie store (where the salespeople have extensive training). Know that you're likely going to need to try on several bras to find the brand that works best for you. The good news? Taking the time to track down a great-fitting bra will (literally) take a load off your chest.

WHEN YOU GO SHOPPING BRING ALONG THE CLOTHING YOU PLAN ON WEARING WITH YOUR NEW BRA

If you're looking for your bra to work with T-shirts, then bring your T-shirt with you. If you're looking for a bra to wear with a dress that dips low in the back, then bring that dress to the store so you can make sure it works.

SCHEDULE TIME TO GO BRA SHOPPING WHEN YOU'RE NOT IN A FRANTIC RUSH

And, just like bathing suit shopping, try to shop earlier in the day when you feel your skinniest. I put shopping for undergarments in the same wildly annoying and time-consuming basket as bikini and jeans shopping, but once you've got it right, you'll be able to establish which brands work best for your body. Going forward, you'll cut your shopping time in half. Not only that, here's why it's so important to find the right bra: over time, breasts that aren't properly supported can sag, resulting in stretch marks. And if you're full-busted and don't wear a supportive bra, you can cause permanent damage to your neck, back, and shoulders.

IF YOUR BOOBS ARE SPILLING OUT OVER THE CUPS (or out of the sides), your bra cup size is too small and you need to go up a cup size. It does not mean you need to go up a band size—a mistake many women make.

THE BEST WAY TO PUT YOUR BRA ON is to lean forward, let your breasts fall into the cups, then stand up straight and fasten the back.

IF THERE IS GAPPING IN THE BRA CUP, it means it's too big, and you'll need to go down a cup size.

IF YOU TAKE OFF YOUR BRA AND CAN STILL SEE THE OUTLINE OF IT ON YOUR SKIN, it's too tight. And I'm astonished you can still breathe, actually. You need to go up a band size.

IF THE BAND ACROSS YOUR BACK FORMS AN UPSIDE-DOWN "V" it's because the band is too loose. Go down a size in the band width so that it sits tighter and straighter across your back.

MAKE SURE WHATEVER BRA YOU BUY FITS COMFORTABLY ON THE LOOSEST HOOK AT FIRST, so you can move it to the tighter ones as the bra stretches over time with wash and wear.

UNDERWEAR DRAWER ESSENTIAL
LACY, SEXY BRA FOR EVENING

WHY YOU NEED ONE

This one is your pretty, feminine bra, and every woman needs one to amp up her WOW FACTOR. A few suggestions on how to wear it: sexy bras work ingeniously under evening attire, like a deep V-neck dress, or a menswear-inspired shirt unbuttoned daringly low. They also work well under stiffer fabrics like cotton, linen, or wool. Just don't wear it under anything flimsy or sheer that allows the lace to show through the fabric (übertacky) and keep away from a lacy demicup style (which only covers the bottom half of the breast) under anything snug-fitting because it can make your bust look divided into four parts.

For an average bust:
LE MYSTÈRE ISABELLA ALL OVER LACE
I love this one because of its memory foam cups that mold to your breasts without any push-up. It also exposes just enough boobage for sexy tops without being trashy. (Tempting but not tacky is the idea.) Plus, the sweetheart neckline is flattering on everyone.

For the busty:
PANACHE ANDORRA SUPERBRA
This bra is great because it's got plenty of support for a large bust, but is also insanely sexy and completely comfortable. It comes in sizes all the way to an H cup.

For the small-busted:
VICTORIA'S SECRET BOMBSHELL BRA
I defy anyone to create push-ups better than the geniuses at Victoria's Secret. Seriously, this one will add two full cup sizes for major cleavage and delicious fullness that any starlet would covet.

EVERYDAY T-SHIRT BRA

WHY YOU NEED ONE

A T-shirt bra might be the most boring one in your collection, but it's probably the one that you'll get the most use out of. This bra should be full coverage with completely smooth soft cups or molded cups (I recommend molded to my clients to give more definition) and minimal lace detailing so that your T-shirts or clingy knits slip smoothly over it. Get at least one skin-toned and one in black. You never need a white bra. A skin-toned bra vanishes under clothes; a white one screams out its outline. And always wear a black bra under black clothes.

For an average bust:
BALI ONE SMOOTH COMFORT-U BACK UNDERWIRE BRA
Just enough coverage, and the molded foam cups give a totally natural outline without making you look like Dolly Parton. Get one in nude and one in black.

For the busty:
PARFAIT BY AFFINITAS "JEANIE" PLUNGE MOLDED BRA
This bra goes up to a 40G and it's lightweight, comfortable, and has super supportive wide straps that don't dig into your shoulders. Le Mystère's Dream Tisha 9955 is another classic fave for my full-busted clients.

For the small-busted:
MAIDENFORM CUSTOM LIFT TAILORED T-SHIRT BRA
This is the best-selling push-up bra in department stores. No bulky, fake-looking pads here, just a totally natural-looking lift. As your cup size goes up, the inner pad goes down to give you a looks-like-you-were-born-with-it perky lift.

STRAPLESS BRA

WHY YOU NEED ONE

A strapless bra is truly invaluable. I hand them out to every client in the summer to wear under all those spaghetti-strap, flimsy, or off-the-shoulder tops. So many clients claim, "But I'm too busty to wear a strapless bra!" Not so. Mistakenly, most women assume that they need the support of straps to hold up a bra, but it's actually the support that comes from the underwire that holds up your breasts. Look for strapless bras with stay-put rubber overlays around the bands, and ones that come with convertible straps so you can turn them into racer back or halter styles and triple the bra's usefulness.

For an average bust:
JEZEBEL LACE ATTRACTION STRAPLESS BRA

I wore this on live TV for a New Year's Eve countdown under a one-shoulder gown, so I needed to make sure there was no telltale outline. The gripper strips around the underwire make it super secure, and it goes up to a DD.

For the busty:
VA BIEN ULTRA LIFT PERFECT STRAPLESS BRA

I love this one; it's got three hidden "stays" sealed between the layers of foam in each cup to lift your breasts. Double silicone on the elastic of the top and bottom keeps the bra in place and gives you that extra support.

For the small-busted:
LE MYSTÈRE SCULPTURAL STRAPLESS

My clients with smaller busts love this one, as it gives a gradual lift for totally natural-looking cleavage and is wildly comfortable. It's got great support, plus a deep plunge for low-cut tops. It comes with removable straps, so you can wear it as a regular bra as well (bonus!).

WHY YOU NEED ONE

Shapewear has come a long way from the corset-like underpinnings granny suffered in. Today's super sexy, supremely comfy pieces are designed to be worn daily under everything (and are under the exquisite clothes of every supermodel and celeb). The secret is a thigh slimmer. Look for medium control (so you don't feel like a stuffed sausage), high-waisted (so you avoid the muffin-top look) and ones that extend to midthigh (for knee-length dresses) or to the knee (for ankle-length). When sitting, check that it doesn't peek out from the hem of your dress. I've seen unsuspecting celebs interviewed on a sofa with all eyes focused on telltale thigh slimmers—a career-ending gaffe for their stylists.

INSIDE SCOOP

For the average woman:

WACOAL ANTI-CELLULITE IPANT LONG LEG SHAPER

This is my go-to secret piece. I hand one to clients to wear under any fitted dresses or thigh-clinging skirts. Insanely comfortable, it smooths you out from your tummy to your mid-thigh. Look for laser cut edges to avoid any dreaded leg bulge.

For fuller figures:

BODY WRAP THE CATWALK HIGH-WAIST +

My fuller-figured clients adore this one because its panels have different levels of tension that help maximize the slimming effects, so you feel fully supported. It's also incredibly comfortable and goes up to a 3X.

Finally someone figured out that shapewear by body shape is a brilliant idea. Enter Wacoal's Control Freak Shapewear Collection: shaping briefs designed with your body shape in mind. There's a brief that's perfect for a **COCKTAIL RING,** proportionately designed for a fuller waist and hips with panels to help lift the butt and smooth out your midsection, and another ideal for a **FRAGRANCE BOTTLE.** This brief is designed for fuller hips, with a more relaxed leg opening to leave room for a curvy bottom half.

SPORTS BRA

WHY YOU NEED ONE

You might not be running a marathon (can you believe that I actually ran one? Wearing Chanel lipgloss all the way!) but you still need support for any exercise. A good sports bra needs to fit snugly but not feel too tight, and it should cover your breasts completely. Look for smooth, moisture-wicking fabrics, and stay away from anything with a high percentage of cotton, since it sops up sweat and stays wet. Look for fabrics like Coolmax or DriFit, which stretch, dry quickly, and retain their shape. It should have nonabrasive, smooth stitching that lies flat. Since your boobs can travel up to 8 inches when they bounce (eek!), jog in place in the dressing room to test out how it feels before you buy.

Got big boobs?
CHAMPION DOUBLE DRY+SPOT COMFORT FULL-SUPPORT SPORTS BRA

Memorize this: the larger your bust size, the less stretch and the more coverage you need. Look for separate bra cups that hold (rather than squish) your breasts, and wider shoulder straps that adjust at the front rather than the back (easier to get to).

Got small boobs?
CHAMPION SHAPE T-BACK SPORTS BRA

For a small size, more stretch is fine. Grab the rib band and strap to see how elastic it is. Give it a good yank. More compression will mean it's more comfortable for higher-impact activities, so find something slightly molded with an adjustable hook enclosure.

FITTED CAMI

WHY YOU NEED ONE

One of the insider secrets that I use the most is the decidedly unsexy cami. This innocent basic has the power to transform those complicated pieces you don't know how to wear into items of clothing you cherish. Soon you won't know how you ever managed without one. Got a shirt that's just a little too sheer? A skin-toned cami underneath makes it wearable. Bought a cardigan that you never know what to pair with? A cami in a coordinating shade will anchor it. Have a work blazer that dips a little too low? Slip a cami underneath and head to the boardroom in confidence. Look for camis with built-in bras if you're less than a C cup, or slip one over a T-shirt bra if you're fuller-busted.

For an average bust:
COSABELLA TALCO LONG CAMISOLE

If you're an A or B cup, you'll wear this endlessly under just about everything. It's got a built-in shelf bra (so you don't need to bother with another bra underneath) and it comes in twenty-five shades. And the longer length is great since it doesn't reveal any flabby tum.

For the busty:
SPANX SIMPLICITY SCOOP NECK CAMI

Love this one because the neckline has darts that release compression and flatter your bust, and it's got nice wide straps (so you can wear your bra underneath). Plus, it's got a full-coverage back for extra support.

GETTING DRESSED

WHAT TO WEAR UNDER WHAT

One of the questions I get asked most is what to wear under all those complicated-looking tops and dresses that you see on the runway. The fact is that most models have pinpricks for boobs, rarely need a bra, and if they do, we double-stick tape them everywhere on the day of the shoot. In real life, you want to be able to wear all kinds of clothing with different necklines and fabrics. Here's what I teach my clients about what should lie beneath.

BACKLESS

↓

LOW-BACK BRA

FREDERICK'S OF HOLLY-WOOD BODY SCULPT BACK-LESS BRA
I swear by this one for any dramatic, backless dress. The adhesive silicone cups (with underwire and replaceable clear wings!) have enough support for a DD cup, and you can reuse it twenty-five times.

RACER-BACK

↓

T-BACK BRA

MAIDENFORM CUSTOM LIFT T-BACK BRA
Spot-on perfect for any racerback top. This one's a favorite because it has removable push-ups so you can decide if you want more or less "boobage."

OY-CUT BRIEFS

MATCHING SKIN-TONE BRA

SKIRT SLIP

PLUNGING- NECKLINE BRA

COSABELLA 24/7 MID SLIP

Who would have thought a half slip would be invaluable? But they truly are. Wear one under any skirt that you're pairing with tights so that the skirt hangs perfectly without clinging to your legs.

COSABELLA AIRE LOWRIDER HOTPANTS

Just in case the wind picks up and you don't want to reveal chubby buttocks in a thong, go for a fuller-cut panty instead. Find one that's semi-sheer, seamless, and has enough coverage. I love these.

MY SKINS T-SHIRT BRA

A bra has to match your skin tone if you want it to be invisible. If it's white or black, it will show through anything sheer. This one comes in twenty different shades, so it does a disappearing act under just about anything you might put on.

LE MYSTÈRE BARDOT SUPER-LOW PLUNGE PUSH UP BRA

Look for ones like this that have a very low front closure, instead of a wider band. Without any extra push-up, it's got wide wings for added support and doesn't dig into your armpits.

SOLUTIONS FOR UNDERWEAR DILEMMAS
JACQUI TO THE RESCUE

Of the hundreds of makeovers I've worked on over the years, these questions and complaints pop up again and again.

MY LARGE BUST MAKES ME FEEL FAT, EVEN THOUGH I'M NOT OVERWEIGHT. WHAT CAN I DO?

So here's the thing about big boobs: Instead of looking sexy, showing too much cleavage can potentially make you look older and heavier. Not only that, but you can easily veer into the vulgar category if you insist on push-ups and demicups. The key is to allude to a sensational bustline without going over the top. Less is more when it comes to classy cleavage. The power of intrigue is extremely sexy.

If you're large-busted, reserve the push-ups and demis for the bedroom, and ramp up your vamp appeal with pretty, feminine bras that have fuller coverage and straps that lift and separate the "girls" to instantly swipe ten pounds from your frame. My go-to brands for fuller-busted clients? WWW.PANACHE-LINGERIE.COM, WWW.FREYALINGERIE.COM, and WWW.FANTASIE.COM all make sizzlingly gorgeous bras that range from a D to a KK cup.

I'M AN A CUP AND HAVE ZERO CLEAVAGE BUT WANT IT. WHAT CAN I DO?

Add these words to your lingerie vocabulary immediately: underwire, gel cushion, push-up. They all help to create the illusion of a fuller bust. Firm, supportive cups will give you unfailing confidence in whatever you're wearing, without making you feel self-conscious that your boobs are wearing you. But make sure the bra fits both breasts perfectly, so you're not spilling out from the sides (if you are, go up a size in the cup).

Look for bras that lift and separate, which gives the most youthful appearance. Brands that specialize in creating spectacular va-voom? Victoria's Secret has the insanely-sexy-add-major-volume-to-your-bust market covered better than anyone else on the planet. However, it's not all about bigger-is-better: I shop for my smaller-busted clients at sites like WWW.THELITTLEBRACOMPANY.COM, WWW.ITTYBITTYBRA.COM, and WWW.LULALU.COM.

MY BUST SIZE FLUCTUATES EVERY MONTH AND I CAN'T AFFORD TO BUY LOTS OF BRAS. WHAT CAN I DO?

Up and down a size every month? You're not alone. Look for bras in stretch fabrics with shape-to-fit technology that are specifically designed to stretch and recover to conform to your fluctuating bust needs (a super smart yarn!). The Bali Comfort Revolution Wirefree with Smart Sizes Bra comes in four sizes (S, M, L, and XL) and makes finding the right fit goof-proof.

I HATE MY BACK FAT. IS THERE ANYTHING I CAN DO?

Yes, I know. I've heard it a gazillion times, which is why I always bring this out whenever one of my clients rears the ugly back fat conversation: Shapeez Unbelievabra Tankee Short. It's an ingenious cross between a body-shaping cropped cami and a bra that miraculously smooths away any back fat. Voila!

TOP 5 LIES
ABOUT LINGERIE

NO ONE CAN SEE THOSE CLEAR, INVISIBLE PLASTIC BRA STRAPS.

Everyone can see those clear, "invisible" plastic bra straps.

THIS HOSIERY IS TOTALLY RUN-RESISTANT.

Yeah, right. (And Titanic was unsinkable.)

THIS ONE, VERSATILE BRA WILL WORK FOR EVERY OUTFIT.

Sure, if you plan on wearing the same, exact outfit every day.

YOU CAN'T FIND PRETTY LINGERIE FOR PLUS-SIZE BOOBS.

Not true. There are a gazillion gorgeous brands for full-figured girls.

WEARING A BLACK BRA UNDER A WHITE TOP IS A TREND ANYONE CAN PULL OFF.

Carrie Bradshaw was wrong. This is not for you.

CONFESSIONS
FROM THE CONFIDENTIAL FASHION FILES

When I was younger, I worked at an advertising agency in central London, and my subway stop was serviced by an antiquated lift (yes, London is deliciously old). One morning I was running horribly late for work, and I wriggled my way into the packed elevator of harried office workers just as the doors snapped shut behind me. It took about thirty seconds for me to realize with horror that the hem of my midlength peasant skirt had caught in the elevator doors and was slowly ripping off to reveal my chubby legs in knee-length granny knickers.

As the doors opened, I had to back out nonchalantly, clutching my skirt around my bum as I ran as fast as I could (in heels) to my office. The moral of this story? Always wear underwear you don't mind showing the world in a (humiliating) emergency.

And maybe wait for the next lift.

WHAT'S IN STORE?

SHOP LIKE A PRO ONLINE OR IN HEELS

Okay, the truth: I hate shopping. (Which means, out of necessity, I've become brilliant at it.) So if you're like me, have no time and a busy life, and just want to pick up exactly what you need instead of browsing leisurely, then, my darling, read on.

The first rule? Shop with an action plan. Stores are positively evil about using tricks to persuade you to part with your hard-earned cash. Take stock of what you already own, and don't get sidetracked. Remind yourself that you already have fourteen navy tees. And be specific about what you might need: a blazer for work, a black belt for those favorite pants, or a classic trench that goes over everything.

Having focus means filtering out pieces that don't flatter your shape (remember what you already learned in Secret One?). Yup, you may have fallen in love with that blush-colored chiffon cocktail dress, but you'll (a) probably wear it once at most because the shade makes you look like a cadaver, and (b) it'll showcase every bump and bulge. So admire it, recognize how delectable it is, but realize that it's not for you and store it in the back of your mind for one of your slender, olive-skinned friends who'll work it to its deserved advantage. You see, the secret is this: Don't waste another nanosecond on what doesn't work for your body or your life. Oh, and lastly, don't buy anything on sale that you wouldn't love at full retail. Let's hit the stores…

…AND SCORE YOUR BEST BARGAINS EVER.

WHO

FASHION EDITORS SHOP WITH

Personally I prefer to shop solo. I'm far better at scoring bargains as a lone ranger (most stylists think this way because, for us, shopping is a job). But if you do take along a friend, keep these rules in mind:

BE SELFISH

Ask a friend to join you as your fashion consultant, or vice versa. She should have absolutely ZERO interest in shopping for herself. I know this isn't what you want to hear, but I've learned that it's practically impossible for two women to shop together and be remotely productive. Go with a friend if neither of you needs anything and you're just window shopping on a lazy Saturday. But if you both need something specific, it's too demanding to fully satisfy both your needs: You'll feel guilty and she'll feel frustrated that you're trying on your twenty-seventh black dress.

TELL YOUR FRIEND IF SHE LOOKS UGLY

Cruel, I know. But friends don't let friends buy anything that makes them look fat. If she's trying on a less-than-flattering dress, tell her honestly that it might not be her best choice. (And now that you know your body type as well as hers, you'll be a far better shopping buddy.) I promise there's a way to gently encourage her to step away from the dress, and she'll thank you later. She's put her trust in you for an honest opinion, so tell her the truth.

LEAVE THE "PROFESSIONALS" OUT OF IT

It's tough to find sales staff who give a truly honest opinion. They often work on commission, and may steer you toward something that's not the best choice so they can make their quota for the day. I'd love to believe they have your best interests at heart when they're squeezing you into a skin-tight dress and assuring you that the zip struggling to close will easily go up at home, but the fact is, they may be thinking about their commission instead. Find someone unbiased who can offer a frank opinion without any financial motives.

WHAT

STYLISTS WEAR TO GO SHOPPING

An unfussy HEADBAND to keep hair tidy

An easy-to-slip-off TUNIC TOP for the changing room

A CROSS-BODY BAG for hands-free browsing

Stylish and comfortable LEGGINGS

SLIP-ON SHOES without zips or buckles

DON'T LOOK LIKE A BAG LADY

Take the time to look simple but polished. When you look wealthy you get better service. If your hair is long, wear it in a stylish ponytail.

AVOID THE STORM

If at all possible, try not to shop in a thunderstorm, when you have to contend with the additional bulk of rain boots and an umbrella.

DO SOME UNDERCOVER WORK

Bring the bra you plan on wearing to make sure it works with the item you intend to buy.

BE READY TO STRIP

Don't dress for a shopping trip in anything with fiddly buttons, time-consuming side ties, or tight boots that are a struggle to put on and take off. Avoid necklaces that can easily tangle, and go with a cross-body bag so your hands are free to browse the racks.

DON'T EVEN THINK ABOUT WEARING THESE

Blister central! And far too complicated to put on and take off.

BRING HEELS AND A STRAPLESS BRA IN A LIGHTWEIGHT TOTE

If you're trying on anything fancy, you can see exactly how it will look.

WHAT

STYLISTS DO IN THE FITTING ROOM

AND WHAT THEY DO BEFORE THEY TAKE THE TAGS OFF

HOG THE FITTING ROOM

Find the biggest room they have. You'll need plenty of space to stand far away from the mirror and get a look at yourself from all angles. Before you join the line for the changing room, gather at least three sizes of the same item so you're not forced to rejoin a lengthy line. Remember: fewer items and more sizes on hand equals less time in the changing room and a higher success rate. Once you try on an item, move around as much as you can in it. I see busty women all the time buying dresses that look great while they're standing, but the instant they sit, their boobs push up and spill over à la Pamela Anderson. And take a good look at yourself from the back in a three-way mirror—a crucial step many women skip.

KNOW WHEN TO WALK AWAY

If the item is too complicated or fussy and you're not sure how much use you'll get out of it, don't buy it. If you need an instruction manual or an engineering degree to work out how to wear it, don't buy it. If the collar sticks out or itches, don't buy it. If you want to tuck it in and it doesn't quite tuck into the pants you're wearing, chances are it won't tuck into your other pants, either. But most important, if it's too tight, don't buy it hoping that you'll lose weight. It has to work for you now—and should just need a few tailoring tweaks to be near perfection. I have a rule for all my clients: they're only allowed to buy something if they can convince me how much they love it (and I'm a tough sell) and describe at least three other items in their closet they'll wear it with.

Don't remove tags until you actually wear the piece. It's better to leave it hanging in your wardrobe with the opportunity to return it for store credit than have totally wasted your money. Try on your new duds with the clothing you'd planned to wear with it in the comfort of your own home and in your own mirror. If you decide it doesn't work, find out the store's return policy—most offer store credit even if they don't give you a full refund. So, while I know it's tempting to rip off the tags immediately to marvel at your conquest, refrain until you are 100 percent certain.

WHAT
STORES DON'T WANT YOU TO KNOW

No one in "the biz" is telling you about how the stores are
tricking you into buying more rubbish that you don't need, but here are
a few phrases that should raise your perfectly arched eyebrows…

WOULD YOU LIKE A FREE MAKEUP APPLICATION?

This is how makeup consultants lure you. They're delighted to chat as they spend hours applying layers of eye shadow when you were only browsing for concealer. Once they're done and have assured you how this puce shade brings out your hazel eyes, you feel wildly guilty about how much time they've invested. So you buy everything.

CAN I START YOU A DRESSING ROOM?

It's one of the top tricks employed by sales staff to make you lose track of how much you're considering spending. If your arm is no longer weighed down by thousands of dollars' worth of bulky sweaters, you're far less likely to realize that you're shopping like someone on a spree. And if they offer you "refreshments and something to snack on" you know that you're not getting out with your credit card intact. Once you're fed and refreshed, they know that you'll stay longer and try on even more stuff.

YOU'RE INVITED TO OUR VIP EVENT!

Store events that make you feel like an insider, such as "Most Valuable Customer Day," are an ingenious way of tempting you to spend on purchases you'd probably never normally consider. The stores know that making you feel like a VIP will entice you to spend like one—and they're right. If there's champagne, a DJ and hors d'oeuvres on offer, they'll have you hooked…and spending.

EVERYONE WANTS THOSE!

Salespeople know how to play off your insecurities and sell you the "hot ticket" item. The next time you pick up a bag and the saleswoman says, "Oh those bags are just flying off the shelves! Everyone's been coming in and asking for them and it's the last one," don't be swayed. Unless it's in your budget and is exactly what you intended to purchase, don't believe the hype.

WHERE
TO SHOP

OFF-PRICE AND OUTLET STORES

It's disarmingly easy to be lulled into believing you're scoring the deal of the decade, but while bargains can certainly be found at outlets (fertile hunting grounds for fashion editors and private stylists) the rule of thumb is Buyer Beware. Yes, every once in a while you'll find a stellar deal. The real treasures at these off-price stores are the end-of-season or marked-down designer pieces that were in the designer's boutique just a few weeks ago, but as a result of surplus or excess inventory have now found themselves in the outlet store. (Yay!) Keep in mind that designers have become much smarter with their manufacturing and supply chains and have learned to make more accurate amounts.

Here's another fashion insider secret: Off-price retailers struggling to find surplus inventory to sell will often ask designers to specifically create clothing that seems like a bargain. So while you might think you are scoring a huge discount on something that would otherwise be outrageously expensive, it may not be the case. Designer brands might manufacture a blouse in the same style as you'd find in the designer's store, but create it in a lesser quality fabric and trimmings (think 20 percent silk instead of 100 or plastic buttons instead of mother-of-pearl ones) specifically for the outlet.

If the original piece is "Made in Italy," take a look at the label in the outlet to see if it was "Made in China" (much cheaper to produce). Be wary of pieces that look "off" or suspiciously different than the ones in the mainstream version of the retailer.

BOUTIQUES

If there's a local boutique where you love the merchandise, ask to meet the store owner. They're often happy to update you when new products and brands arrive, and can be on the lookout for items from a particular designer you like. Store owners are also useful resources to keep you up-to-date on hot trends, and if you spot a great brand in another store, ask your buyer if they'd consider carrying it in the store for you.

DEPARTMENT STORES

Department stores can be overwhelming, so familiarize yourself with the layout via a store map (get one from the information counters in most large department stores) to make your shopping more efficient. Ask a salesperson specific questions about which floors carry which types of merchandise. I like to shop with my clients first thing in the morning: the sales staff are generally bright-eyed and bushy-tailed, and the dressing rooms are usually emptier.

CONSIGNMENT STORES

You can score incredible deals at a consignment store. The secret: shop in wealthy areas where you're likely to find top-quality, unworn designer pieces with original price tags attached. (I've had clients send $30,000 worth of never-worn pieces to a local consignment store!) Be prepared to try clothes on in the store, since some pre-owned items may have been altered by a tailor. Hunt for trend-resistant staples like statement jewelry or designer handbags, or one-off evening gowns you'd never be able to afford otherwise.

STYLING STORE WINDOWS

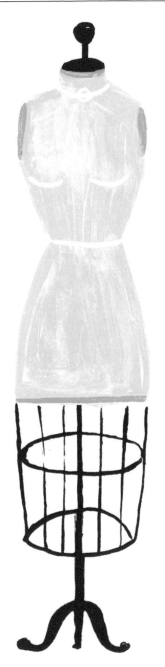

Clients often ask me about styling mannequins and window displays, so take a close look at one next time. Mannequins are meant to show off the clothes to their full advantage, which is why mannequins are likely to be wearing two or three layers at any one time, simply so the stores can display as much of the merchandise as possible. **A TYPICAL STORE MANNEQUIN TODAY IS A SIZE 4 WITH A 20" WAIST AND A TYPICAL SHOPPER IS A SIZE 14 WITH A 34" WAIST, SO THE REAL WOMAN IS GOING TO LOOK AN AWFUL LOT BULKIER IN ALL THOSE LAYERS.** A store mannequin might look great in a tank layered under a long-sleeve tee. Over that, there'll be a shirt with at least four necklaces and over that might be a long-sleeve jacket, layered over a vest. She may also be wearing a hat, holding a handbag, and have at least two pairs of socks peeking over her ankle boots. (Exhausted? I am.) But obviously you don't need to dress like that in real life. They just want you to buy everything you see.

WHEN
TO SHOP

THE SEASONS

Timing is everything. Fashion people know that shopping for seasonal, trend-resistant staples (like trench coats for spring or winter work pants) should be done off-season so that you can save big. Spring clothes hit the stores in January, so don't stock up on everything you need for spring right away. Wait until April to buy your classic lightweight looks, and you'll save a bundle. You can still get a bit of use out of them in the remainder of the season, and there's always next year.

THE HOURS

Women always ask me about the best time of day to shop. Usually the answer is whenever you have a free minute. But, if you can, try to shop super early in the morning. First thing on weekday mornings is always the best time to get serious shopping done. You're filled with energy, the lines are shorter at the register, and the sales assistants are ready and waiting to help you locate the sizes you need.

THE MONTHS

It's tempting to buy something that you can wear right now. Who doesn't love instant gratification, right? But once you make the shift from the way you normally shop (right before the season begins when everything has just hit the stores) to the way savvy fashion editors shop, it will become second nature. On the next page, I've put together a fashion editor's calendar just for you.

INSIDE SCOOP

Around the holidays, fashion editors are often "gifted" designer wallets or bags (especially if they've been generous throughout the year with their editorial coverage). If you happen to live in or near a major metropolitan city, January might be a great time to scour your city's consignment stores for fabulous leather goods that may have been discarded by a fashion industry insider who has received one too many Chanel wallets. (Though can you really have too many?)

WHAT TO BUY WHEN

JANUARY

TEMPTING TO BUY: The newest spring trends and resort pieces that work brilliantly for a hotspot vacation like kaftans, bathing suits, and flirty dresses in spring shades.

WHAT FASHION EDITORS BUY: Outerwear. Score a classic peacoat for next year. (And it's likely still cold enough to wear now.)

FEBRUARY

TEMPTING TO BUY: Spring blazers to layer over long-sleeve tees and a new raincoat that you can probably get use out of right now.

WHAT FASHION EDITORS BUY: Classic winter accessories like hats, scarves, gloves, and boots, all reduced for the end of the season.

MAY

TEMPTING TO BUY: Beach items. Stores want you to stock up on sandals and bikinis.

WHAT FASHION EDITORS BUY: Scour the sales racks for heavy-weight knits and cashmere sweaters. (They're a fraction of the price now.)

JUNE

TEMPTING TO BUY: Summer tees and tanks to layer on weekends.

WHAT FASHION EDITORS BUY: Spring sandals start to go on sale, and you can still get several months' use out of them with your pretty summer dresses.

SEPTEMBER

TEMPTING TO BUY: Cooler-weather clothing, like long-sleeve tops, denim jackets, and blazers.

WHAT FASHION EDITORS BUY: Summer travel accessories: think beach totes and insanely useful weekend bags.

OCTOBER

TEMPTING TO BUY: Heavier-weight knits, sweaters, and winter pants.

WHAT FASHION EDITORS BUY: Lightweight transition pieces (like cotton jackets) to bring out the nanosecond the winter freeze thaws next spring.

MARCH

TEMPTING TO BUY: Spring shades of denim (like cobalt, coral, and lime) to tuck into boots, and lighter-weight cardigans and sweaters.

WHAT FASHION EDITORS BUY: Fragrance. Score on any gift with purchase promos, like a luxury travel-sized body lotion or shower gel in your signature scent.

APRIL

TEMPTING TO BUY: The first deliveries of pretty summer dresses to start wearing with bare legs.

WHAT FASHION EDITORS BUY: All the resortwear (like kaftans, shorts, and lightweight tunics) left over from the January spring deliveries.

JULY

TEMPTING TO BUY: The very first fall deliveries and the newest fall shades. Denim colors move toward olive, wine, and mustard.

WHAT FASHION EDITORS BUY: Swimwear and sandals, deeply discounted because there are only four weeks of "summer" left.

AUGUST

TEMPTING TO BUY: The newest fall bags for "back-to-school," or a tote to impress your coworkers at that fancy corporate office.

WHAT FASHION EDITORS BUY: Floaty, summery dresses. Anything with spaghetti straps or that requires bare legs will soon be out of season and therefore much cheaper.

NOVEMBER

TEMPTING TO BUY: Outerwear like coats and boots.

WHAT FASHION EDITORS BUY: Jeans. Everyone's gearing up for the holiday season, so the denim market is flat. Take advantage of slashed prices.

DECEMBER

TEMPTING TO BUY: Holiday dresses and major bling for all those WOW-worthy parties.

WHAT FASHION EDITORS BUY: Bridal. No one is dress shopping in December for their big day. Get in on the sample sales, where prices are slashed up to 80 percent.

Hello Jacqui   Shipping to: **United States**   Help | Privacy & Cookies | Sign in | My Wish List 11 | Register   (Empty) SHOPPING BAG

2
3

THE OUTNET

THE MOST FASHIONABLE FASHION OUTLET

JUST IN   DRESS ME   DESIGNERS   CLOTHING   BAGS   SHOES   ACCESSORIES — **1**

Home > Designers > Calvin Klein Collection > **Festi jersey dress**

CALVIN KLEIN COLLECTION
Festi jersey dress

NOW $238 Original price $528 **55% off**

Select a size: **Italian sizing** Size charts — **8**

36   38   40   42   44   46   48

ADD TO BAG >

ADD TO WISH LIST — **7**

Color: Merlot

Details & Fit — **4**

• Calvin Klein Collection merlot Festi dress
• Heavyweight jersey
• V-neck, stitched pleats, fully lined
• Slips on
• 71% viscose, 21% polyamide, 8% spandex
• Dry clean
• Fits large to size. Take one size smaller than normal — **5**
• Semi-fitted style
• Mannequin height is 180cm/ 5'11" and is wearing an IT 38

Need advice? Contact Customer Care
Product code: 233527

Measurements — **6** +

Designer Information +

Delivery & Returns +

Like   Tweet   Pin it   Send   +1

Click image to zoom — **10**

9 — You may also like...   Wear it with... — **11**

J.W.Anderson
Leather biker jacket
with quilted sleeves

Alaïa
Cutout leather sandals

Alexander McQueen
Faithful leather tote

THE OUTNET
About us
Advertise with us
Why shop with us?
Your feedback
Careers

DESIGNERS
Alexander Wang
Hervé Léger
M Missoni
Marni
Shop designers A-Z

DRESS ME
Weekend
Date Night
Work
Cocktail Hour
Wedding
Luxe Traveler

HELP
Contact us
Payment & Security
Shipping information
Returns policy
Terms & Conditions
Privacy & Cookies

SIGN UP FOR SHOPPING UPDATES
Enter email...

Affiliates | Advertise with us | Sitemap
© 2009-2012 THEOUTNET.COM

KEY

1 Don't limit yourself by shopping by designer—shop by category and you might discover a new label.

2 Register for e-mail alerts to be notified about new arrivals.

3 Follow on Twitter or "like" the retailers' Facebook pages; it's the best way to find out about promotions.

4 Read the size and fit notes carefully. (If it's shot on a model, she'll likely be taller than you, so the hem might hit in a different spot.)

5 Some sites make recommendations about whether you need to go up a size or if something should be worn fitted or loose.

6 Don't ignore product measurements.

7 Love an item but still waiting for pay day? Keep track of it via wish lists.

8 Use size conversion charts. Designers use UK, French, Italian, Danish, and Japanese sizing. Websites like WWW.THEOUTNET.COM show you how to convert to your U.S. size.

9 Sold out in your size? Look for other options you might like just as much.

10 Use zoom functionality to get a closer look at the fabric.

11 Check out how items have been styled for suggestions of what to wear it with.

INSIDE SCOOP

Instead of signing up for brand newsletters that you probably ignore, "like" the Facebook fan pages of your favorite brands or follow them on Twitter, since the PR reps post insider online deals immediately. And if you buy something online and it goes on sale a few days later on the same site, call them to ask for a price match. Many reputable online retailers will offer you a credit for the difference.

HOW
FASHION EDITORS SHOP ONLINE

Ah, the allure of online shopping. No-limits shopping, 24/7.
I've been known to browse for clients in the middle
of the night or during a boring TV production meeting.

READ THE FINE PRINT

Little appeals to shoppers like the promise of free shipping. But beware, online buyer: shipping isn't cheap, and the cost is usually covered elsewhere. The most common method retailers use now to make up the difference is a minimum purchase requirement.

The downside is the temptation to add unnecessary purchases to qualify, goading you to spend more than you'd planned. Look at the total cost before you buy. Factor in the time it would take to go to the actual store and shop, how much shipping is, and how easy it will be to return. . Think before you check out.

IGNORE THE "STELLAR" PRODUCT REVIEWS

First, read between the stars. Look for details about the product, which are a much better indicator of whether or not this is a high-quality product that fits what you need. Another trick? Look up the item on Google images to get multiple views to give you a better idea of what it looks like, and read buyer reviews on multiple sites.

Many sites censor their reviews, and if all the items have five stars or the tone of the reviews seems oddly sales-oriented, this should raise suspicions. High-end major department stores tend to have the most reliable customer feedback, so if you're shopping on a smaller site or boutique, try to look up the item at a department store, just to be sure.

KNOW THE REAL COST OF RETURNS

As convenient as online shopping is for consumers, you can't try on the clothes that you're buying, which means a lot of returns. (Repeat returners can even get banned in some cases.) Know the return policy before you purchase. Some e-tailers offer easy postage-paid returns, but some don't.

CHOOSE SITES THAT ALLOW YOU TO NARROW YOUR SEARCH BY SIZE

This is a useful trick to stop the temptation to buy something too big or small just because you love it.

READ THE SIZE, FIT, AND CLEANING CARE NOTES CAREFULLY

That white dry-clean-only silk dress might not be such a bargain if it's spending half its life at the cleaners.

CONFESSIONS
FROM THE CONFIDENTIAL
FASHION FILES

I, too, have succumbed to the perils of wickedly expensive shopping mistakes. My fondest memories involve being abroad and dealing with a foreign currency, which seems to make over-spending that much more forgivable. (Especially if you're really bad at math.) One time I bought a navy (yes, school-marm-navy), dowdy, midi-length, silk skirt from a wildly expensive designer in Sydney, Australia, because I couldn't work out the currency conversion quick enough and was too humiliated to snatch back my credit card. Or the time I was seduced by the Bambi-limbed beauties at MaxMara in Rome and was persuaded to buy a skirt suit that, once I got back Stateside, I realized made me look like a stuffed sausage.

The thing is, I got swept up in being on vacation. We always think this is the only chance or a one-time opportunity, and that's a dangerous mindset to have when shopping.

SECRET

5

WORK THE CATWALK

TURN RUNWAY INTO REALITY

Ah! Those fashion trends. How the industry loves to torture us mercilessly each season. It's all about the maxi. No! A midi! No! A mini! (Trust me, I understand your frustration.) But here's a universal truth: genuinely stylish women don't fall prey to trend traps; they add their own unique twist to what you spot on the pages of a magazine. As a non-negotiable rule, if you look like you're trying too hard to be fashionable, you'll never look chic. When it comes to trends, women tend to fall into two distinct camps: those who slavishly follow them and those who feel entirely left out of the fashion conversation so they just give up altogether.

In this chapter, I've taken a few of my favorite perennial runway trends to show you how absolutely everyone—of any age and body type—can wear them to WOW!

So whether you're sixteen or sixty, boobalicous or flat as a board, I'll show you how to master animal prints, leather, florals, denim, and stripes—and work them to your advantage. Horrified by florals? Think you could never pull off a mini past 40? Too timid for animal prints? I'll show you how to rock any trend, no matter what your body type. So let's take a jaunt down the runway…

...AND LEARN HOW TO FLAUNT THOSE HARD-TO-WEAR FASHION TRENDS.

ANIMAL PRINTS

You can guarantee that one version or another of an animal print shows up on the runway every single season. But the truth is **ANIMAL PRINTS CAN GO SO RIGHT, OR OH SO WRONG.** And if you've always shied away from incorporating them into your wardrobe, terrified because they're so, well…LOUD, then I'm here to show you that this eye-catching print is a great way to add a dash of sizzle to any look. (They're also a surefire way to veer into "working girl" territory if you get it wrong, so less is definitely more.) But first things first: the closer the print looks to the actual animal, the higher-quality the garment will appear. And rather than wearing it head-to-toe (like our gorgeous friend to the left), animal prints work best when paired with a neutral solid so that the print is the main focus. Animal prints work ingeniously to draw attention to the parts of your body you love, so embrace them to highlight great shoulders, shapely legs, or your enviably tiny waistline. Here, I've sorted it all out for you by your body shape.

So fabulous, I can't stand it! I'm obsessed with the swing coat, the dress, the bag, and the booties. But maybe a little over-the-top unless you're on a catwalk.

FRAGRANCE BOTTLE

LIPSTICK

HEART PENDANT

SUNGLASSES

COCKTAIL RING

MAKE IT LOOK UPSCALE

Wear the print on your top half to draw focus upward. A sheer animal print top or a bolero are great examples of attention-grabbing pieces that highlight your shoulders and upper body. Pair with a darker-colored skirt or pants to downplay heavier hips and thighs.

GO SAFARI

Your slender body shape can easily pull off this curve-enhancing print in a head-to-toe, figure-hugging dress. Just keep all other accessories to a minimum. (Put down those crazy earrings and skip the larger-than-life Vegas hair.) Add classic shoes: a simple nude pump works best.

SEXY BUT CLASSY

Embrace the print on the bottom half only please, my voluptuous darlings. Too much boob + leopard print is a definite no-no (and looks cheap no matter how much you paid for it). Stick to a skirt or boots to showcase sensational legs and keep everything else as simple and subdued as possible.

GET PLAYFUL

With your body shape, you can pull off an animal-print trench or wrap dress beautifully. In fact, anything that nips in at the waistline will work. One of my classic style tricks: anchor a crisp white shirt and work-appropriate pants with an animal-print belt that enhances your curves.

JUST A TOUCH

Animal prints work perfectly as accents and help distract from problem areas (like your lack of waist-line). Embrace them in accessories: a slender silk scarf, which can also be looped through the handles of a classic tote, or a sexy, chunky-heeled, leopard print pump that pulls eyes downward.

LEATHER

A little bit bad girl, but a whole lot of fabulous. Leather in a simple silhouette looks effortlessly chic.

Ah, leather, **THE UNIFORM OF THE REBELLIOUS.** Ever-present as the very essence of cool, leather can look pitch-perfect or punk gone horribly wrong. Every body shape can embrace leather, as its stiffer structure tricks the eye into creating the illusion of the perfect silhouette. Without being goth, punk, or metal, here's how any shape can rock it.

FRAGRANCE BOTTLE

LIPSTICK

HEART PENDANT

SUNGLASSES

COCKTAIL RING

THE BOMBER LOOK

A cropped leather bomber will add dimension and width to your top half. Look for wide lapels and exaggerated shoulders that broaden your upper body and help reduce your bottom half. Leather reflects the light, so use it to draw eyes upward. · Please, promise me you'll never be tempted by leather pants.

PARTY IT UP

Use leather's stiff structure to create more curves than you really have. A fitted bodice or a dress with a corset-like top will boost your bustline, and a slightly flared shape will give the impression of a curvier bottom half.

A CHIC UPTOWN LOOK

You, beautiful girl, were the reason they created leather skirts, and it's one of the best fabrics to balance out a fuller bustline. The gentle A-line shape and the fabric's sheen draw all eyes to your bottom half and lend welcome balance to a bustier top.

CHANNEL YOUR INNER ROCKER

A sexy sheath dress gets unexpected edge when it's made of leather. Wear this as the only vamp item in your outfit and keep everything else simple. You can also embrace leather in the form of a fitted vest over a classic button-down to show case your waist.

AN URBAN STYLE

Create a skinnier waistline with a longer, tailored blazer worn open. This will draw attention toward the center sliver of your frame and away from its width. Pair with dark-wash jeans and a pair of heels for a longer, leaner silhouette.

FLORALS

One of the most versatile prints, florals can be so docile yet so intimidating. **FLIRTACIOUS FLORALS AND PETALS ALWAYS POP UP A GAZILLION TIMES ON THE SPRING RUNWAYS,** but I'm often surprised by the number of women who shy away, believing they'll end up looking like wallpaper—or worse, their mother. But florals can be your best friend if you pick the right bloom for your body type. Whether it's a dainty Liberty of London-type tiny print, an edgier, more abstract one, or simply rosettes clustered on a shoe or a clutch, there's the perfect petal for your shape.

Trust me, my darling,
the right bud for you is out there,
I promise.

FRAGRANCE BOTTLE

LIPSTICK

HEART PENDANT

SUNGLASSES

COCKTAIL RING

BOLD BRIGHTS

Whether you go for splashy vibrant shades or more muted florals, the key is to bring the focus to your top half. A nipped waist/ flared bottom dress works brilliantly to conceal hips and thighs. If in doubt, look for a bold floral print on top and a small, delicate print on bottom.

BODY-HUGGING BUDS

Wearing prints is one of the easiest ways to add dimension to a straighter shape, so you can pull off a body-con, watercolor floral easily. Pair this look with nude accessories to allow the print to be the focus.

CALI-CASUAL PRINT

A bold, attention-grabbing print on your bottom half will balance out your figure and showcase great legs. Pair with a fitted V-neck in a solid color.

FEMININE FLORALS

Dainty florals on a cap-sleeved, waist-cinching dress highlights your hourglass shape. Or embrace florals as an accent— thread a slim floral silk scarf through your belt loops in lieu of your usual leather belt.

SUBDUED PATTERNS

Keep the print in proportion with your frame. Dainty, girly florals might disappear on you, so look for floral prints that are clustered vertically and placed more toward the center of your body to make your torso look narrower.

DENIM

Head-to-toe denim?
Looks fabulous on this chick,
but…no.

The once-humble blue jean now comes in such a vast array of styles and prices that the choices can be dizzying even to a die-hard fashion expert. **IT SEEMS THAT EVERY SEASON AN ENTIRELY NEW, NEVER-SEEN-BEFORE DENIM SILHOUETTE EMERGES,** urging us to dash out and purchase the skinny! The bell! The boot! But wait, you think, I look like Hettie Heffalump in skinny jeans, and the bell shape seems far too frivolous. Which designer should I really be following now? And they cost how much? Is that a joke? Never fear, my denim-clad darlings. I'm here to clear up all your blue jean blues and teach you how to make the denim trends work for your shape.

FRAGRANCE BOTTLE

LIPSTICK

HEART PENDANT

SUNGLASSES

COCKTAIL RING

POLISH YOUR LOOK

Balance your lower half with a bootcut style in a dark wash—they'll hug your thighs and flare out from the knee. Go for a clean front and flat pockets (or have them removed by a tailor). Look for back pockets placed high and angled inward to make your butt look smaller.

CHANNEL AUDREY HEPBURN

Rather than baggy boyfriend jeans, go for skinnies or legging styles that hug your narrow hips and calves. Pockets with embellishments—flaps, buttons, or grommets—placed high on the butt amp up your assets and give the illusion of more bum than you have.

THINK BOHO CHIC

Go for a wider-cut leg, instead of a skinny leg (which throws you even more out of proportion). Opt for a mid- or low-rise cut, since they'll help extend the length of your torso. Stick to lighter washes, which create the appearance of volume without bulk.

IMAGINE VINTAGE

Look for a higher-waist cut to emphasize the difference between your waist and hips, and a gentle flare to keep you from looking top-heavy. Go for yokes (the seam at the back, below the waistband) with a deep V, instead of straight across, to highlight the curve of your butt.

GO CASUAL AND CLASSIC

A dark-wash, straight leg shaves off inches. Look for jeans with a curved waistband that follows the line of your waist, and a higher rise to offset fuller hips. Opt for lighter fading along the center panel and side seams that sit slightly inward, to help whittle your legs even more.

STRIPES

This trend has its own striped past, with its history as everything from a pattern for prison garb to its reemergence as a regal, nautical trend. In my opinion, **THE HUMBLE STRIPE IS LARGELY MISUNDERSTOOD.** Whether you go for nautical, pinstripe, fat stripes, or skinny ones—trust me, there's a stripe for you. It's all about width and placement. Eyes are drawn to wherever the print lies on your body. I'll show you what I mean.

{ **INSIDE SCOOP**

Ever wondered why news anchors rarely wear stripes on TV? It creates an optical illusion called moiré or "strobing," which makes viewers' eyes go fuzzy. I learned that lesson while I was filming a show in Hong Kong and wearing a striped tee, and countless viewers called in feeling nauseous. }

See how the bold stripes are creating such a sensational shape?

FRAGRANCE BOTTLE

LIPSTICK

HEART PENDANT

SUNGLASSES

COCKTAIL RING

CLASSIC AMERICAN

Midwidth horizontal stripes and a boatneck will make your shoulders look broader and offset fuller hips and thighs. The key is to keep stripes above the bum. Pair a striped top half with a solid-navy bottom to downplay your lower body.

BOLD IS BETTER

The wider the stripe, the bigger you'll look. Which is why fat, horizontal stripes flatter a straighter frame by adding figure-enhancing dimension. Also, look for interesting color placement: see how the thick red stripe across the hip area of this sweater helps create the illusion of a curvier shape?

THINK SKINNY

Embrace a skinny stripe (even a horizontal!) that's placed wide apart. A thicker stripe would overemphasize your bust, as large stripes magnify. Go for slim-fitting shapes with V-necks to elongate your neckline.

BIG IS SEXIER

Form-fitting knits or tops with thick stripes will showcase an hourglass shape beautifully. Or embrace the menswear trend that looks sexiest: a striped shirt that peeks out from the top of a collar or from the hem of a solid-colored cardigan. A closely fitted long-sleeve tee will also work perfectly on your womanly shape.

STRAIGHT UP

You're probably the most fearful of stripes, right? Don't be. Go for slimming vertical ones that draw the eye up and down, and break up the pattern by wearing them inside a solid cardigan or jacket. This way, the stripe draws eyes away from the sides of your body and inward toward the center of your frame to great slenderizing effect.

FASHION TRENDS

Fashion moves fast. Colors change (Hello neon-green, goodbye tangerine) and silhouettes morph (Waistlines are here! No! Wait, now they're there!). But looking your best is always on trend. Here, a timeline of some of our timeless faves.

600 B.C.

The cavewoman look is totally in and **ANIMAL PRINT** is all the rage. (It never stops being trendy.)

1853

The gold miners need pants that are strong (and don't tear easily) to withstand searching the mines during the gold rush. Loeb Strauss starts a wholesale business supplying pants made of **DENIM.** He later changes his name from Loeb to Levi.

1937

Women's fashion is introduced to the nautical look when Coco Chanel is photographed wearing a **STRIPED** sailor top and khakis.

1952

Roman Holiday is released, and Audrey Hepburn's **HEADSCARVES** spark a trend among young girls. Bernard and Laura Ashley fall in love with this trend when they are on holiday in Italy. They begin to produce their own small scarf collection. Within a short time they're selling millions.

1953

The **LEATHER** jacket achieves iconic status when Marlon Brando dons one as Johnny Strabler in The Wild One. Many years later, the Fonz's iconic leather jacket from Happy Days is laid to rest in the Smithsonian.

1971

Ralph Lauren opens a boutique in Beverly Hills for both men and women. It features his aristocratic style at prices the average American can afford and creates a sensation. In his designs he favors natural fabrics and patterns with a **WESTERN** or country motif.

1987

Madonna's single "Like a Virgin" is released. It marks the beginning of Madonna as a fashion icon for young women around the world who want to emulate her **"STREET" LOOK** with lace, crucifix jewelry, and bras worn as outerwear.

1990

It's all about **GRUNGE.** Flannel shirts, frayed, light acid-wash jeans and androgyny are all the rage. Think white T-shirts, Nirvana, and Doc Martens.

2008

Michelle Obama is the first African-American First Lady. For such an iconic global moment, she wears a black and red Narcisco Rodriguez **SHIFT DRESS,** with a black satin cross detail at the waist. Her sleeveless dresses cause controversy all over the world, but she soon becomes a fashion icon to rival Jackie O.

2011

Prince William and Kate Middleton marry on April 29 at Westminster Abbey. Young women every-where want to emulate the new Duchess of Cambridge's **MODERN YET CLASSIC LOOK.**

INTERPRETING TRENDS AT ANY AGE

This is a great time to bring up age. Age is just a number, but what you get away with in your twenties might not be as appropriate (or flattering) when you hit your fifties. Maybe your skirts are just a smidge longer now, but your sexy options are certainly not limited. In fact, certain style statements age like fine wine and get infinitely better with time. Instead of talking about how to go from miniskirt to muumuu, let's look at the essential pieces to don for every decade of your wildly fashionable life.

SLEEVELESS DRESSES AND TOPS

You're likely to have slender, toned arms, so work them to their best advantage with one-shoulder looks that showcase a pretty décolletage.

IMPRACTICALLY HIGH HEELS

You probably don't have the style constraints of balancing a baby on one hip or racing to your kid's soccer game. Go ahead and dash around town in sky-high heels.

TRENDS TO LOOK FOR IN YOUR

20s

Now's the time to be bold and brave with fashion (and make lots of mistakes you can laugh at later). Experiment with color, heels, and hemlines.

RUFFLES AND SHEEN

While a girly top might look too frivolous in your thirties or forties (without at least the addition of a blazer), a babydoll style at this age works brilliantly paired with skinny jeans.

HIGH TREND FASHION

Colored skinny jeans, faux fur vests, fedoras, neon, studs. Now's the time to embrace every passing trend, my darling. The key is this: less-pricey brands instead of designer pieces. The trend will pass.

COCKTAIL DRESSES

Invited to more upscale affairs than when you were younger? Source a few stand-out cocktail dresses that flatter your figure in shades other than yawn-worthy black. Pair with statement accessories like killer heels and a great clutch.

CLASSIC-CUT JEANS

Still into whiskering, fading, acid-wash, or rips? No, no, no, and no! Give them to your little sis and replace with a bootcut, dark-wash pair that you can just as easily wear to the office on casual Friday as you can with a sexy animal print.

TRENDS TO LOOK FOR IN YOUR

30s

Start building a more classic wardrobe of essentials that work as hard as you do: professional looks for the office and dresses for date nights.

TAILORED PANTS

You really can't beat a beautifully tailored pair of flat-fronted charcoal or black pants to pair with a crisp white shirt and heels for work. Dress them down for weekends with a snug tee, a cropped denim jacket, and ballet flats.

MATERNITY DRESSES

Preggers? Sorry, but there's absolutely no excuse to drown your growing baby bump in oversized, shapeless muumuus. Pieces in fabrics like form-fitting stretch jersey will grow as your baby does and ensure that you look stylish pre-, during, and post-pregnancy.

SHIRTDRESSES

Flattering on most body shapes, a fitted menswear-inspired shirtdress is a fuss-free way to look boardroom-ready in a cinch. Pick a solid shade and pair with statement earrings and a bold cuff.

FITTED BLAZERS

Little is more versatile than a tailored, fitted blazer. A slim-lapel, single-breasted blazer can be worn as part of a suit for day. For night, just push up the sleeves and add jeans and heels.

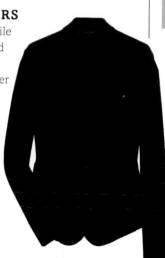

TRENDS TO LOOK FOR IN YOUR

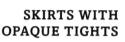

Like your love life, you've probably figured out what works for you (and what doesn't!) Find quality pieces with clean lines and interesting cuts.

SKIRTS WITH OPAQUE TIGHTS

Less-than-perfect legs? You can still embrace above-the-knee skirts or dresses easily if you wear them with dark, opaque tights. Match your shoes to your hosiery and your legs will look miles long.

BOOTS AND PUMPS

The simplest way to add a youthful touch? Invest in eye-catching boots or pumps to turn the plainest outfit into a style statement. Just be wary of heel width: Chunkier heels help thicker calves look slimmer, while kitten heels and skinny stilettos look best on thinner legs.

TEXTURE
Instead of super trendy colors, add visual interest with varying textures. Think leather, crocodile, patent, fur, or vinyl—all fresh, unique ways to keep a mono-chromatic outfit looking one-of-a-kind.

COLOR
Light-reflecting, softer shades worn close to your face— like pinks, ivory or pale lemon— will help brighten your complexion and bring welcome luminosity.

TRENDS TO LOOK FOR IN YOUR

50s

Now you know for sure which trends work for you. You're going for quality over quantity, and using light-reflecting, age-defying color to your advantage.

BOLD COLLAR SHIRTS
Feel that your neck is aging you? Go for shirts in pale shades, like ivory or white, with stiffer funnel collars. Avoid wearing a shawl around your shoulders to hide your neck.

BOLD ACCESSORIES
You have enough gravitas to pull off strong accessories without having them wear you. An oversized statement piece like a cocktail ring or a bold necklace keeps your style looking fresh without looking fashiony.

BELTS

Belts are basically age-resistant. Whether it's a glossy patent leather or an embellished fabric, a belt (nipped over a slim-fitting cardigan, or worn with a tailored pant) defines your waistline and adds a finishing touch to the simplest look.

CARDIGANS

Not your granny's sweater twinset. Wear a fitted cardigan with your favorite pants. Go for ones with interesting trim or unusual buttons that add a fresh twist on a classic item.

TRENDS TO LOOK FOR IN YOUR

60s

The biggest mistake women make in their 60s? Getting trapped in a style rut. Tame cutting-edge fashion trends by embracing just a touch—a ruffle here, an embellished trim there…

COATS

A tailored overcoat in a bold, solid shade is a quick way to lend a youthful look to your outfit. Go for coats that hit at the knee, the most flattering length for most women.

OVERSIZED SUNGLASSES

A must-have accessory for the sixty-and-over set. Look for glasses with skin-flattering frames and lenses: a tortoise-shell is universally youthful-looking.

TOP 5 FASHION LIES
ABOUT TRENDS IN THE MEDIA

EVERYONE IS WEARING IT.

I've lived all over the world and Americans are particularly—and often perplexingly—
obsessed by this concept. In other parts of the globe, trends don't catch on
like wildfire the way they do in New York. Not only is the use of "everyone"
an overstatement, but who wants to look like everyone else anyway?
Rock your own interpretation of the trend and set yourself apart from the herd.

YOUR SKIRT/TOP IS SO LAST YEAR.

Skirts and tops are in every year. If the garment is still in great shape (and you still love it),
there's no reason to toss it just because you read an article that told you that look was
"so five minutes ago." Chances are that it's just the silhouette that's changed,
so get yourself to the tailor and hike up that hem, or add a belt to make last year's
skirt and top look like this year's brandnew dress.

IF YOU DON'T WEAR THE TREND, EVERYONE
WILL THINK YOU'RE OUT OF THE LOOP.

No one should ever wear anything out of fear—only love,
as in "I'm in love with how this trend looks on me."

I WORE THAT TREND THE FIRST TIME AROUND,
SO I CAN'T WEAR IT AGAIN.

This is actually a sad reason to ignore a trend. Just because you wore
bell-bottoms in 1970, doesn't mean you can't get the updated version now.

YOU CAN SPEND ON THIS TREND, BECAUSE
[insert ridiculous trend here] **WILL BE IN FOR A WHILE.**

Trends are ever-changing by their very definition. And fashion must
continually change in order to survive. Don't feed the beast.
Save big on trends, and spend only on classic pieces.

CONFESSIONS
FROM THE CONFIDENTIAL
FASHION FILES

I can't tell you how many times I've gotten it horribly wrong by slavishly following trends in my youth. As I've gotten older (and wiser) I've learned that there are things that I'd just love to be able to embrace (like bum-scraping miniskirts), but since I don't have the legs for them, I step away. It would also be entertaining to swan down the street in wide-legged tuxedo pants (a terrible idea, as I'm so short), flirty shorts (laughable!), or delicate, sparkling sandals with ankle-wrapping straps (that would just make me look like an ungainly gladiator instead of a Capri-bound starlet). But the fact is, I can't carry off these trends—so I don't. However, I can wear a gazillion other fun trends that different body shapes can't. So please, learn from my mistakes. Friends don't let friends dress like disasters.

SECRET

6

STRIKE IT RICH

DRESS
WEALTHY
EVEN IF
YOU'RE NOT

If you've ever wondered what makes someone look wealthy, then this chapter is for you. Want the secret formula for looking like a gazillion bucks? Read on. After years of styling the super rich, I've analyzed the common denominators they all share. Want to look like you're dressed head-to-toe in couture? I'll show you how. Or a key accessory that makes a world of difference? It's in this chapter.

"Why should I bother to 'dress rich'?" you may well be asking. Because, while it's a harsh, bitter truth, when you're dressed with a dash of sophistication, you're treated better everywhere. It's just a brutal fact, my darlings, that when people think you've got money, your stock rises. Yet "looking moneyed" has zero to do with how much you have in the bank. It's about mastering those few subtle tricks that will lend your look an aura of extreme wealth, understated elegance, and exceptional taste. You don't need to set foot near Tiffany's or Harry Winston, my friend. I'll unravel the enigmatic rules for looking wealthy…

...AND REVEAL THE INSIDE SCOOP ON
LOOKING REALLY, REALLY ELEGANT.

RULE NO. 1

FAKE A CLOSET FULL OF COUTURE CLOTHING

So exactly what is it that makes someone's wardrobe look wealthy? The secret is this: it's all in the colors they choose (subdued or jewel tones, never overly trendy, garish brights), the fabrics (they've never heard of polyester), and the stylish yet discreet finishing touches in accessories.

PICK THE RIGHT
COLORS AND PRINTS

If you peeked into the closets of my clients, you'd be hard-pressed to find any neon-pink, citrus-green, or acid-yellow. Instead, there's a carefully cultivated palette of taupe, aubergine, sapphire, and emerald. (A rule of thumb: If a color sounds like an expensive jewel, it will probably look like an expensive color.)

They also embrace shades like chocolate-brown, camel, navy, charcoal, burgundy, cream, and winter white. Rather than buying cheap-looking, loud prints, invest in something timeless, like plaid or herringbone. Designer devotees layer on texture, so combine different fabrics—like satin, fur, or leather—in the same color family.

PICK THE RIGHT
FABRICS

For fabric, a higher price point indicates a better yarn. Look for clothing with a high percentage of luxurious, natural fibers like silk, cashmere, wool, and cotton. Synthetic, man-made yarns like polyester or nylon will look and feel less high-quality.

PICK THE RIGHT BELT

Rich women worship their belts. A slender leather one in tan, chocolate, black, or a faux-exotic skin (like alligator or python) pulls together an outfit and makes you look instantly polished. Go for one with an expensive-looking finish and solid hardware. Splurge on a designer brand and save on everything else.

RULE NO. 2

FAKE A FINE JEWELRY COLLECTION

It's all in the details. Rich people have figured out that a few well-chosen accessories make a dramatic difference. But you won't find any teen-inspired, gimmicky pieces. (Put away anything featuring rubber, plastic beads, skulls and crossbones, or Hello Kitty.) Instead, stick to classic pieces that will stand the test of time.

WEAR LESS BLING,
MORE SPARKLE

Looking chic and expensive is all in the details. If you can't afford real diamonds, don't wear giant fake ones that couldn't possibly be authentic. If you go for the daintier fakes, no one will suspect they're anything but bona fide half-karat diamonds or precious gems.

INSIDE SCOOP

A men's watch worn on a woman's wrist has a cachet all of its own. Feign ridiculous wealth with an oversized, undeniable classic like Tag Heuer's 1969 Monaco.

FAKE IT 'TIL YOU MAKE IT

The quickest way to look like you've got a ton of cash? Blend spectacular eye-catching pieces with inexpensive ones. Everyone will automatically assume that each piece is a designer brand. For example, an instantly recognizable style statement like a sparkling Swarovski crystal necklace could easily be paired with a few slim bangles that cost practically nothing. Yet the overall effect? Call it wealth by association.

RULE NO. 3

FAKE LUSTROUS, SHINY HAIR

Ever noticed how wealthy women seem to have unbelievably lustrous, thick hair? They may have the time and funds to schedule regular trips to the hair salon (and pamper themselves with luxurious conditioning treatments infused with flakes of 24 karat gold), but you too can have fabulous hair with these insider tricks.

GET TRIMS AND
BLOWOUTS REGULARLY

A healthy eating regimen can help give you the glossy hair you've been coveting. Look for foods that contain Biotin (a B vitamin that helps strengthen hair and nails), such as nuts, eggs, and Swiss chard. And omega-3 fatty acids are anti-inflammatories that help hair grow, so eat a diet rich in flax seeds, walnuts, and healthy-fat fish like salmon and tuna. Healthy hair also comes from scheduling regular trims every four to six weeks.

Hunt down an inexpensive salon where you can get a smooth, full-bodied blowout as often as you can afford. (Blow-dry-only salons, like Blow or Dry Bar are popping up in major cities and offering speedy, reasonably priced blowout services only, instead of more expensive full-service salons.) Shine-enhancing treatment products, like Rita Hazan's Foaming Clear Gloss, a lightweight treatment that boosts shine with vitamin B5 and silk amino acids, can be used as needed. Use your favorite conditioner each time you wash your hair and once a week apply an at-home intensive conditioning treatment. Try Pantene's Pro-V Daily Moisture Renewal 2-Minute Moisture Masque, which is formulated with a concentrated dose of conditioners that penetrate the hair to keep it moisturized, nourished, and supple.

ADD SHINE

Get a bottle of Moroccanoil Treatment (or its sister for people with baby-fine hair, like me—Moroccanoil Treatment Light). Run a quarter-sized blob through wet hair without touching your roots, then style as normal. It makes hair look shiny as glass, and keeps it smooth and frizz-free all day.

Another shine secret? Stylists swear by a bracing cold water rinse. Too brutal to contemplate in winter? Just dip your ends in cold water in your sink.

INSIDE SCOOP

Try an at-home hair-straightening regimen for super smooth hair. Bumble and Bumble's patent-pending Concen-Straight Smoothing Treatment loosens curly bonds and realigns them into smoother shapes and lasts for up to thirty washes. John Frieda's Frizz-Ease 3-Day Straight is a weightless spray that helps seal in straight styles for up to three days.

RULE NO. 4

FAKE COSMETIC SURGERY

Their glowing skin is flawless (neither a fine line nor a brown spot in sight) and their smile reveals Chiclet-white teeth. They've got that fresh glow of apple-cheeked youth. Why? Because rich women can afford to get all that aging sun damage reversed by a plastic surgeon or at a dermatologist's office. Here's how to score the same results...from the drugstore.

HIDE SUNSPOTS

Wealthy women have derms on speed dial for skin-perfecting chemical peels and laser resurfacing. My clients stock up on BB cream (a blemish balm), which is a cross between a tinted moisturizer and an anti-aging cream. BB creams help soften, smooth, and refine, while encouraging skin rejuvenation. (Try celeb derm Dr. Brandt's BB Cream with Flexitone.) Downplay any wrinkles on your forehead with side-swept bangs, and swipe away decades instantly.

LOOK LIKE YOU'VE HAD AN
EYE LIFT

Brows should be luscious, full, and natural, as harshly penciled or skinny ones look cheap. Truly perfect arches will make you look as if you've had an eyelift. To find the ideal placement of the highest part of your arch hold a pencil parallel at the outer edge of your iris. Makeup artists often dab a hint of highlighter just under the arch to open up the eyes even further.

LOOK LIKE YOU'VE HAD YOUR TEETH WHITENED BY A
CELEBRITY COSMETIC DENTIST

You can pay upward of $500 for professional teeth whitening at the dentist or you can use an at-home whitening system from the drugstore that uses the same enamel-safe ingredients. Up to you. (Crest 3D White Intensive Professional Effects Whitestrips show results after just one use.)

LOOK LIKE YOU'VE HAD
COLLAGEN INJECTIONS

Dab a dot of cream highlighter on top of your lip's Cupid's bow and in the center of your bottom lip. Shiseido's The Makeup Accentuating Color Stick in Glistening Flush S3 is what's used by makeup artists backstage. Or put gloss just in the middle of the bottom lip to reflect the light.

FAKE A PERFECTLY
SCULPTED NOSE

Dip an angled brush into foundation that's a couple of shades darker than your skin tone and draw two lines down each side of your nose. Use a lighter shade to draw another line down the center of your nose. Then blend, blend, blend. Make Up For Ever makes a Sculpting Kit with two compact powders for this very purpose.

RULE NO. 5

FAKE A FABULOUS LIFESTYLE

Whether it's a leisurely day browsing glossy magazines at the spa or a luxury pedicure in a rose-petal-strewn glass bowl, rich women never skimp on treating themselves to the best pampering treatments around. But who cares if you don't have the same bank balance? Here, the inside scoop on how to look like a million bucks.

LOOK LIKE YOU JUST GOT A FACIAL

It's all about exfoliation. Get an at-home facial cleansing system that helps slough away dead skin cells to reveal brighter, smoother skin instantly. Olay Professional Pro-X Advanced Cleaning System includes a rotating cleansing brush and a gentle, lathering formula that delivers derm-worthy results for a fraction of the cost.

WHAT RICH-LOOKING WOMEN ASK FOR AT THE NAIL SALON

Keep nails short, just to the tips of your fingers, and file them into a square shape with softly rounded edges. If your nails chip easily, go bare and rub cuticle oil over your nail bed for a manicured look in seconds. Eschew trendy nail shades and instead stick with the classics. For an everyday, nude-ish pink try Essie's Ballet Slippers (a whitish pink) followed by a swipe of Mademoiselle (a super sheer pink) on top. Other time-tested classics: Merino Cool, a mid-shade brown that flatters all skin tones, Jazz, a toasty nude that's a bit hipper than pale pink, or Chinchilly, an understated gray that looks achingly sophisticated.

LOOK LIKE YOU HAVE LAVISH COSMETICS

Treat yourself to items that might be seen in public for touch-ups: a gorgeous lipstick case, a glamorous compact, or a pretty designer gloss—but get your basics from the drugstore. Apply a drugstore-brand lipstick as a base at home and bring out the fancy gloss in public. You never see rich people whipping out a half-chipped powder compact with crumbling blusher falling everywhere, do you?

LOOK LIKE YOU JUST CAME BACK FROM VACATION

Fake a visit to St. Tropez with a goof-proof, fast-drying, self-tanning treatment that's impossible to mess up. Jergens Natural Glow Express Body Moisturizer gives a believably healthy glow in just one day and deepens to a full shade in three days.

FIVE EXPENSIVE ESSENTIALS

1 STRUCTURED

My wealthy clients never wear oversized, shapeless clothing. Even the handbags they tuck over their arms are structured, polished, and perfectly sized. Expensive-looking clothes are designed with strong infrastructures and have a shape even when you're not in them.

2 SMALL

When it comes to looking wealthy, small and discreet is always better than big and brash, regardless of where you bought it. Stay away from overt displays of wealth like obvious designer logos (particularly tacky if you wear more than one at a time). Truly wealthy women aren't ostentatious when it comes to their extravagant purchases.

3 SUBTLE

Understated is key. Take hair color, for example. Rich people have hair colors that are found in nature. (No harsh zebra stripes or startling shades that make you look like a poor version of Lucille Ball.) Highlights should be subtle, as if they've come from the sun. Look at pictures of yourself as a child—notice those natural, pretty streaks you got from playing outside? Those are the highlights you should request from your stylist. Pick understated makeup shades, too. Daytime makeup should consist of nudes, taupes, sheers, and neutrals. Lipstick should be just a shade darker than your natural lip color, and blush should match the color of your cheeks when you're flushed (like after a brisk walk). Reserve the vibrant shades (purple, green, cobalt) for evening.

4 SLEEK

Wealthy women look polished and streamlined. Look for cardigans with long, slender lines and intricate piping or seaming. Tailored pieces look couture (even if they're not). If you're wearing jeans, consider a darker, more refined-looking wash. A slim-cut jean tucked into a deep-chocolate or black knee-length riding boot (without any trendy buckles or embellishments) is a timeless and elegant look for winter weekends.

THE TERRIBLE TOOS OF LOOKING CHEAP

TOO TAN

TOO BLEACHED

TOO TIGHT

TOO BRIGHT

TOO MATTE

5 SEDUCTIVE

You might not be able to afford a designer outfit, but you can easily capture a seductive hint of wealth by investing in a classic fragrance, either from your favorite designer or a perfumier you love. Choose a scent you adore and make it your signature. A great way to introduce a little luxury into your life: Splurge on a scented shower gel or decadent body lotion in your favorite fragrance.

THE WORKMANSHIP AND DETAILS

Look at the workmanship and how the seams are finished. Notice how the zippers and buttons have been positioned and try the zipper to make sure it doesn't stick every time you pull it up.

THE FEEL OF THE FABRIC

How does the fabric feel against your skin? Feel the weight of the fabric. Look for heavier weight knitted fabrics (anything stretchy) so they drape perfectly on your body. Then look at the label: Pants made with wool blends, which also have a hint of crease-resistant Lycra, are perfect for sitting in the car or on the train, and are flattering because of that touch of stretch.

As for sweaters, see if it's a cashmere-wool blend and find out exactly what percentage of cashmere. Many fashion brands deliver a "good, better, best" collection for each season. A brand like J. Crew might carry sweaters in merino wool, 100% cotton, and also a premium collection of 100% cashmere.

THE CARE CODE

See if something is dry-clean only, since what seems like a bargain can easily turn into something insanely expensive in the long run. Look for pieces that only need hand washing or can be tossed into the machine on a cool wash.

THE FIT

Clothing quality is especially important if you're fuller-figured. Flimsy fabrics won't lend the crisp tailoring and support you need to create a slender silhouette. Lightweight fabrics can be unflattering to a fuller figure unless you use them as layering pieces. Look for fabrics with stretch or concealed support panels that help hold you in. For more fitted pieces, go for fabrics that recover, bounce back, and don't crease or stick to the body.

THE DESIGNER

Are designer jeans really worth the exorbitant price? The difference between premium denim and a midpriced product is how the denim yarn is constructed, plus its unique finish. Premium denim is created from top-quality yarn and will have the most expensive finishes. Jeans are often hand-finished, with each hole or whisker placed by hand. The quality of the Lycra used will be so robust that it can go through harsh, abrasive washing cycles and still keep the perfect shape on your body. You should be able to sit all day in a great pair of jeans and have them retain the exact fit on your butt and knees. My faves? Japanese fabrics are known to be the best for denim technology.

THE FIT, FIND ONE

Wealthy women don't wear clothes that don't fit. They have a luxurious amount of time to try on everything (or at least everything their personal stylist selects) and every item they own looks as if it were cut specifically for their body. So one of the first tricks to looking wealthy is to get thee to your nearest tailor.

SAVE TIME

You might consider tailoring to be an extravagant indulgence, but a good hemming will be valuable to you. Do yourself a favor and tailor your clothes to your body and your lifestyle. You'll cut your time getting dressed in the morning in half.

FOR DAILY USE VISIT OFTEN

The big misconception is that tailoring should be reserved for fancy cocktail dresses and gowns. However, the trick to looking wealthy is to buy everyday bargain items, like a jacket or a pair of work pants, and get them tweaked to perfection. Buy an inexpensive item like a wool-blend shift dress with a great structure (it should have some shape already) and tailor it to fit to a tee.

FAKE COUTURE

Get your shirt sleeves shortened, request the original hem to be sewn onto your jeans, have dress straps tightened and shirt side seams taken in an inch or so at the waistline. Make sure skirts don't bunch and are just the right length. With a skilled tailor no one will know you've had work done (much like a good cosmetic surgeon), and they'll think you bought it that way. Suddenly, you've created a rich-looking wardrobe on a teeny budget.

A WORD OF CAUTION

Don't rely on tailoring for massive overhauls. If you've lost a significant amount of weight and are down a couple of clothing sizes, reward yourself with a few new pieces. Attempting to dramatically alter what you already have may negatively affect the construction of the garment. Also keep in mind that anything with a lot of overlays, beading, or an asymmetrical style is trickier to fix.

INSIDE SCOOP

How to tell if a man's suit is a custom-made, expensive one? Look to see if the buttons on the sleeve actually fasten, or if they're simply "dummy" buttons sewn onto the fabric. Men with tailor-made suits often leave one sleeve button undone as a subtle signal of wealth. It's a surefire way to separate the men from the boys.

Looking wealthy lies almost entirely in shoes and handbags. Instead of buying a different bag for every day of the week, invest in one exquisite piece (or at least as exquisite as you can afford). Training your eye to recognize what makes something look discount and what makes it look designer is the first step to looking luxurious.

CHI CHI SHOULDER BAG

Expensive-looking bags have structure, classic silhouettes, discreet hardware (no fringe, beading, or overly obvious logos), and top handles. They're neither oversized nor itsy-bitsy, and they nestle perfectly in the nook of your elbow. Wealthy women always seem to carry their bag in the nook of their elbow. Odd, right? Now you'll see it everywhere.

BEAUTIFUL BOOT

A fitted knee-high boot is something that every wealthy woman owns simply because it easily pulls together any outfit. Whether you get a pair in chocolate or ebony suede, tan leather, or glossy patent (be careful with patent though—make sure it doesn't go over the knee, or Pretty Woman might spring to mind), a knee-high boot is a classic that never goes out of style.

CLASSY CLUTCH

For night, invest in a rich-looking clutch in an evening-appropriate fabric like velvet, satin, or jewel-encrusted metallic leather. Go for one that opens easily without any fumbling (more elegant than grappling with a fiddly zipper with a canapé in one hand) and ideally, choose one with a wrist strap so you can sip your Champagne more easily.

FASHIONABLE FLAT

It's the closet staple of the wealthy (or at least every woman along New York's Madison Avenue). Opt for classic ballet flats in vibrant shades of suede, patent leather, or an exotic print. Pair them with slim-cut, ankle-grazing, tailored black pants and a jewel-toned sweater. You'll look like a million bucks.

CONFESSIONS
FROM THE CONFIDENTIAL
FASHION FILES

When I lived in Paris I used to spend weekends with my friends trawling the flea markets ("Les Puces") for unique-looking jewelry that people thought were family heirlooms, like a chunky silver cuff that I've worn to countless fancy benefits and paid just $5 for. Once a TV crew from Japan interviewed me as I came out of Fashion Week and I lied and told them it was a precious antique from Thailand. They believed me. And I've felt guilty ever since.

INSIDE SCOOP

Don't bother with knockoffs—they're giant flags that you can't afford the real thing. Instead, buy a non-designer bag with fabulous stitching, sumptuous-looking fabric, and substantial hardware. When it comes to expensive-looking shoes, look for leather soles, instead of synthetic, and high-quality heel caps, as opposed to plastic, on the base of a stiletto.

BAUBLES AND BAGS

THE EXTRA TOUCHES THAT MAKE A WORLD OF DIFFERENCE

I'm the undisputed Queen of Accessories. I believe that the bits that you add are one of the lowest-cost ways to make the biggest impact. Fashion editors never underestimate the right bags, shoes, and jewelry. Even if you're a jeans-and-tee kind of girl, accessories are the secret to injecting personality or sparkle into your style. The right belt will transform a simple look from dull to dazzling, average to amazing. A statement piece can reinvent a simple top. A vintage addition can catapult a shapeless sheath dress into a compliment-worthy ensemble. A plain blazer (you know, the one you forgot about in the depths of your closet) can be thrust into the spotlight with nothing more than a boldly colored scarf. Even better: accessories are size-resistant. Pick the right one for your shape, and it'll flatter you regardless of whether you gain—or drop— ten pounds.

But how do you navigate the seemingly endless parade of "it" baubles, bags, and shoes? From the three essential pairs of shoes every woman should own to the belts that'll shave inches from your waist, here are the industry tricks what really work…

…AND SHOW YOU HOW SIMPLE IT IS TO GO FROM BLAH TO BRILLIANT.

THE RIGHT NECKLACE FOR YOU

There's no question that **A SENSATIONAL NECKLACE WILL TRANSFORM A DULL OUTFIT,** but with a gazillion styles to choose from, how do you really know which works best? A long, skinny lariat? A bold choker? A chunky statement piece? Stylists know that the secret lies in choosing what works best for your body.

FRAGRANCE BOTTLE	**LIPSTICK**	**HEART PENDANT**	**SUNGLASSES**	**COCKTAIL RING**

LOOK FOR:
Shorter, chunky pieces.

WHY:
Bring attention to your face and make your top half the star of your ensemble.

LOOK FOR:
Bib pieces that sit in the midst of your décolletage.

WHY:
Add dimension to your look and create the illusion of a wider neckline and thus a curvier shape.

LOOK FOR:
Longer pendant styles that hit at the navel.

WHY:
Draw peoples' gaze up and down your torso and away from your bust. (Avoid 16" or 18" ones that perch directly on your boobs like a shelf.)

LOOK FOR:
Shorter, dainty, delicate necklaces.

WHY:
Hint at cleavage and showcase a pretty neckline without overwhelming your curves.

LOOK FOR:
Longer, Y-shaped pieces.

WHY:
Redirect focus from your sides to the center of your frame, making your waist look skinnier.

Fashion editors create outfits and finish the look with exactly the right accessory. You can see it works perfectly, but why exactly? Here is the easiest way to figure out what goes with what.

SILVER WITH COOL TONES

GOLD WITH WARM TONES

Silver jewelry works with this outfit simply because of the dress's cooler shade. If you love silver, pair it with shades like gray, navy, blue-based pinks, violet, and mint green.

Gold jewelry looks fabulous next to this piece, since warmer shades like red, tangerine, bronze, taupe, burnt-orange, and coral pair brilliantly with gold.

THE RIGHT EARRINGS FOR YOU

HOOPS AND STUDS ARE GO-TO CLASSICS. You often see hoops on magazine covers because they're visible under all that fake hair, but you can run the risk of looking like a Mafia mama with giant hoops. So, when in doubt, choose small studs that work with absolutely everything for daytime. Confession: I wear the same pair of stud earrings practically every day. Boring, you say? Nope. It means I can wear statement necklaces and cuffs that don't compete with what's in my ears.

IF YOUR FACE IS
SQUARE-SHAPED

You'll look best in hoops or rounder styles, which help soften angular features.

IF YOUR FACE IS
OVAL-SHAPED

You'll look best in studs, ovals, or teardrops that frame your symmetrical face.

IF YOUR FACE IS
ROUND-SHAPED

You'll look best in longer, chandelier styles that make a fuller face look leaner.

IF YOUR FACE IS
HEART-SHAPED

You'll look best in rounder styles that sit on, or near, the lobe to counteract the length of your face.

There's truly a ring that works for every set of fingers and it doesn't need to match anything you're wearing. **THE SECRET LIES IN MAKING SURE IT'S NOT WEARING YOU** and looks as if it really belongs on your fingers. As a general rule, large-boned hands look better with bolder statement rings and smaller hands and fingers look best in more delicate pieces, like a single solid band or a stack of slender rings. Remember that a beyond-fabulous ring draws attention to your nails, so keep them in good condition. You don't need to bother with an expensive manicure, but people notice the little things like buffed nails and moisturized cuticles.

IF YOU'VE GOT SLENDER FINGERS

You'll look great with delicate, intricate rings.

IF YOU'VE GOT LARGER HANDS

You'll look great with substantial cocktail rings.

INSIDE SCOOP

An easy update for boring shoes? Take a pair of clip-on earrings and slip them onto the front of plain black or nude pumps to make them look completely original.

WHAT BRACELETS TO WEAR

The style secret is to **STICK TO JUST ONE ARM ALONE**; there's little that looks more fabulous than a fat stack of slender bangles snaking up one wrist or a singular, chunky cuff. The easiest, no-fuss solution is to coordinate bracelets within a similar color palette to your clothing, but if in doubt, stick to one shade or one metal. And keep your lifestyle and profession in mind: the sound of jingling and jangling in a boardroom meeting can be really distracting, so you might want to stick to a no-noise piece instead, like a statement cuff.

Bold cuffs look fresh and modern with a plain outfit.

Stack slender bracelets on one arm.

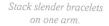

INSIDE SCOOP

For years I've bought ultracheap bangles in small boutiques or street fairs and taken them to be professionally gold-plated for not much more money. Suddenly, an inexpensive metal bangle that cost $5 from a New York street vendor transforms into a glistening gold (albeit plated) piece that has everyone wondering which designer in Paris created it.

HOW TO LAYER JEWELRY

Keep a coherent theme, although overly matchy-matchy sets are a no-no. **DON'T MIX TRENDS**, like layering a delicate, sparkling chain with a chunky skull-and-crossbones choker. Layer varying lengths and materials so the overall effect is casual yet thoughtful, and allow one piece to truly "pop"—a bold cuff on one arm with a stack of skinny bangles allows the cuff to be the standout star. A stylist's secret: pair something generic with something personal, like simple silver bracelets with a cherished silver charm bracelet.

Looks good, right? Same overall theme and feeling.

But here, entirely disparate pieces don't meld together at all!

HOW TO MIX SILVER & GOLD

Be mindful of other accessories with lots of hardware.

Here's the secret—it should look like a deliberate style statement and not as if you just threw on anything and hoped for the best. The contrasts I'm obsessed with wearing together are warm metals like gold, bronze, and copper, and cooler ones like silver, gunmetal, and pewter. Be mindful of other accessories: a tote with an abundance of silver hardware looks at odds with stacks of gold jewelry. Buttons, buckles, or embellishments count, too; a silver necklace over a cardigan with gold buttons looks out of place.

THE RIGHT BELT FOR YOU

This is the most oft-forgotten accessory. **PICK THE RIGHT ONE AND YOU'LL LOOK TALLER AND SHAPELIER;** get it wrong, and you'll look dumpy and wide. The secret lies in choosing a belt that's the right width and wearing it at the most flattering position on your body. The general rule: The bigger your boobs, the lower you should wear it. Only wear belts over clothing with a narrow body-hugging silhouette or over a lightweight silky fabric. (I have yet to see someone who doesn't look fat layering a thick belt over a chunky knit or jacket.)

FRAGRANCE BOTTLE	LIPSTICK	HEART PENDANT	SUNGLASSES	COCKTAIL RING

A 1- or 2-inch belt that sits just below your natural waistline (anything wide or tight on your actual waist will overemphasize a large bum).	A wide belt worn at your natural waistline will make you look curvier.	A 2-inch belt worn low-slung on the hips will open up the distance between your bust and hips and make your torso look longer. The result? A leaner midsection.	A skinny belt worn at your natural waist will showcase your silhouette (without going overboard à la Jessica Rabbit).	A slim belt (1-inch) under an unbuttoned cardigan or an open blazer. You'll just get a glimpse of the belt so it creates the illusion of a defined waist.

INSIDE SCOOP

Why always use the belt buckle when you can just as easily tie the belt in a knot, either centered or slightly off to one side? Try layering two skinny belts in different colors for contrast. Or replace the belt that came with your coat for one in a completely different fabric.

Ah…how we all love to obsess over shoes. How many of us have lusted after delicious leather and suede confections that just beg to be brought home? But do they really work once we've tossed away the receipt? The secret is to **COMPILE A QUALITY COLLECTION OF SHOES WITH HEEL HEIGHTS THAT YOU CAN WALK IN,** that don't require insoles, shoe grips, or toe clenching to keep them on, and that fall within your budget. You don't need to spend your money on designer, you can find quality shoes at a gazillion price levels. But here are the three pairs you MUST HAVE (and are worth splurging on).

WELL-FITTING BOOTS
that you can wear constantly in winter, and that will never go out of style.

BUTTER-SOFT BALLET FLATS
that look effortlessly chic. Chanel, Pretty Ballerinas, and French Sole have endless options.

A SKIN-TONED, HIGH HEELED PUMP
that you can wear with everything and make your legs look longer and leaner.

INSIDE SCOOP

If you want to look taller, wear platforms instead of skyscraping heels. Platforms raise the height of the forefoot off the ground from the inside, so even if you have a 6" heel, it's really only a 4" heel. The thicker your calves are, the thicker heel you need to help balance out a fuller leg. Avoid ankle straps unless you have incredibly skinny legs, because they'll bisect the leg and make you look shorter and dumpier.

WHAT SHOES DO I WEAR WITH...

A SHORT SKIRT	BOOT-CUT JEANS	A WORK SUIT	SKINNY JEANS

↓	↓	↓	↓
WEDGES OR FLATS	**CHUNKY HEELS OR ANKLE BOOTS**	**CLASSIC, HIGH-HEELED PUMPS**	**CHUNKY HEELS OR KNEE-HIGH BOOT**

but don't wear **STILETTOS**	but don't wear **TALL, FITTED BOOTS**	but don't wear **METALLIC EVENING HEELS**	but don't wear **SNEAKERS**
	*You can't tuck boot-cut jeans into them.* 		*Actually, don't ever wear these.*

A COCKTAIL DRESS	WIDE-LEG PANTS	A MAXI DRESS	CAPRIS
STRAPPY SLINGBACKS	PLATFORMS OR WEDGES	FLAT SANDALS OR ESPADRILLES	WEDGES OR BALLET FLATS

but don't wear	but don't wear	but don't wear	but don't wear
ANKLE-STRAP WEDGES	**FLATS**	**STRAPPY HEELS**	**STILETTOS**
They chop off your legs.			

THE ONLY BAGS YOU REALLY NEED

Full disclosure: I own way too many bags. I've either bought them (being in Paris created a horrible Louis Vuitton compulsion) or been given them, but the fact is that no matter how many I own, I gravitate toward the same two over and over. A slouchy Gucci snakeskin tote for day that cost a small fortune and a particularly outlandish Miu Miu mohair clutch for evening that I snagged in the Prada outlet in Milan. So why do I keep returning to these two? Because they work. Here's how to pick your future go-tos.

FOR THE OFFICE

Look for a bag roomy enough for your needs, but structured enough to look professional. Style experts look for bags that are big enough to fit a small evening purse in case they have to head out from the cubicle to cocktails. Neutral shades are the safest (you can't go wrong with black or chocolate), but look for interesting hardware or fresher silhouettes that make you stand out from the pack.

OUT ON THE TOWN

Don't waste your money on something you will realistically carry only half a dozen times a year. Choose a slender cigarette clutch that holds just the essentials for a night out (I find I rarely need more than a lipstick, keys, credit card, and ID), and leave the rest at home. Color-wise, a neutral metallic like pewter goes with practically everything and is more versatile than silver or gold.

FOR THE WEEKEND

Go for long, sturdy shoulder straps—leaving your hands free for running errands or holding little ones' hands—and roomy enough to carry all you need. Look for rubberized canvas outers (better to wipe off dirt) and darker shades that don't get as scruffy or show wear and tear as quickly as paler shades.

BEFORE YOU BUY THAT BAG

ARE THE CLOSURES TRICKY TO OPEN AND CLOSE?

Make sure they're secure enough so things don't tumble out,
but also not so tricky that it takes twenty minutes to open your bag.

DOES IT WEIGH A TON WITH NOTHING INSIDE?

Trust me, it will feel double the weight once you've
added your wallet and the rest of your junk.

ARE THE STRAPS COMFORTABLE?

See that super trendy chain-link strap? Looks fabulous in a magazine,
but wildly impractical when it leaves welts on your shoulder.

ARE YOU A GOLD OR SILVER JEWELRY PERSON?

Make sure the bag doesn't have an overdose of hardware
that clashes with what you normally like to wear.

IS IT SUPER DEEP AND COMPLETELY POCKETLESS?

Could be really annoying when you're trying to fumble for
your phone. Shallower bags tend to be easier to reach into.
Deep bags can end up becoming a "black hole."

INSIDE SCOOP

The fastest way to looking heavier than
you are? A cross-body messenger bag.
Don't go near them if you've got big boobs.
They cut right across your chest and
overemphasize the size of your bust.
A shoulder bag on one shoulder or a sturdy
top-handle bag is infinitely more flattering.

THE IDEAL SUNGLASSES FOR YOU

Here's a little-known secret: The right frames can make you look younger, thinner, and smarter. Yup, they can make people take you more seriously, swipe decades from your age, and pounds from your jowls. Brands are desperate for you to spend a small fortune on a pair, but you don't need to splurge.

ASK THESE QUESTIONS BEFORE YOU BUY

DO THE FRAMES FLATTER MY FACE SHAPE?

Take a look at the hints on the next page to find the sunglasses that suit you best.

DOES THE FRAME COLOR SUIT MY COMPLEXION?

Warm complexions (yellow undertones) work best with khaki-, copper-, or peach-colored frames. Cool complexions (blue or pink undertones) pair better with black, plum, or dark tortoiseshell frames.

DO YOU LIKE THE LOOK FROM AFAR?

Stand in front of a full-length mirror and take a good look at what they look like since sunglasses affect your head-to-toe look.

IF YOUR FACE IS
SQUARE-SHAPED

Got a strong jawline and broad forehead? Go for frames that are slightly rounded at the edges to soften and balance angular features. Ones that sit high enough on your face will downplay the sharpness of your jawline.

IF YOUR FACE IS
OVAL-SHAPED

Oval faces are longer than they are wide and have relatively balanced features. You can get away with most styles as long as the frames are no wider than the broadest part of your face. Cat-eyes, wraparounds, or square styles work brilliantly.

IF YOUR FACE IS
ROUND-SHAPED

Round faces have soft curves with a similar width and length, so find frames with angular lines to add structure. Make sure they're equal to or slightly wider than the broadest part of your face. Dark shades like black or tortoiseshell minimize fullness. Higher temples and details on the brow bar will help create a longer face shape.

IF YOUR FACE IS
HEART-SHAPED

Heart faces are broad at the forehead and cheekbones and narrow at the chin. To broaden the appearance of your chin and bring more proportion to your face, look for lighter gradient lenses (darker at the top than the bottom). The graduated lens tint de-emphasizes a wider forehead while softening the lines of a pointier chin. Aviator styles downplay a broad forehead and narrow jawline.

HOW TO PUT IT ALL TOGETHER

ADD THE WOW FACTOR TO A PLAIN WHITE TEE

Take a plain white tee
and add a bold scarf
+ a charm bracelet
+ sparkly earrings.

ADD THE WOW FACTOR TO AN ORDINARY SWEATER DRESS

Throw on a sweater dress
and add a beaded necklace
+ quirky heels
+ a statement cuff.

ADD THE WOW FACTOR TO A BORING SLEEVELESS TANK

Give your tank some
oomph and add a fedora
+ bold earrings
+ sequined mini.

DD THE WOW FACTOR O WEEKEND JEANS

mp up your jeans with
metallic blouse
animal-print pumps
akes it more evening).

ADD THE WOW FACTOR TO A COCKTAIL DRESS

Get a downtown vibe with
a cropped leather jacket
+ ankle booties (add
opaque tights if you don't
want to go bare-legged).

ADD THE WOW FACTOR TO DESK-TO-DINNER

Transform your work wear
with a sequin tank
+ evening pumps.

BAG THE "IT" BAG

OVERLY TRENDY BAGS DANGLING FROM THE ARMS OF EVERY CELEB

If it's got any sort of over-the-top embellishment like fringe or a crazy color, or its outrageously expensive, don't fall for it (unless money is no object). The fact is, celebs are often "gifted" bags by PR houses in the hope that they'll be photographed with them on their next Starbucks run. Since they're given new bags for practically every event they attend, they don't have to worry about whether it's going to be out of fashion next week.

Most important, don't get swept up into splurging on a limited-edition designer collection (neon Birkins, rainbow-print Louis Vuittons, or glitter Miu Mius are perfect examples). They might light up the pages of a magazine (not to mention the eyes of all the knockoff vendors), but you're better off investing in a classic style and a neutral shade that will never look dated.

THE JIMMY WHO? OBSESSION

RIDICULOUS HEELS THAT COST AN ABSOLUTE FORTUNE

Yes, Manolos and Jimmy Choos have entire TV shows devoted to them (and they're undeniably exquisitely gorgeous), but before you squander your child's college fund, pause to think about how much wear you'll really get out of them. (Trust me, I have spent a small fortune on designer shoes that remain unworn in their box.) And although nothing ruins a spectacular entrance more than heels you can't walk in, fabulous shoes are worth every dime if you can wear them well, so make sure you'll get a lot of use out of them if you do decide to splurge. Choose a shoe that universally has the most flattering cut for your feet: something like a d'Orsay style, which is when the side of the shoe is cut away leaving the arch of your foot exposed, resulting in elongated legs. And shoes with a very low front (toe cleavage!) are insanely sexy.

TRICKY ACCESSORY TRENDS

Can you really get away with the accessory-du-jour? I say, why not?
As long as you're not attempting to look like a teenager.
You may have the body of a starlet, but there are still some
accessories that anyone over thirty looks ludicrous wearing.
Here, some of your most popular accessory dilemmas answered.

Can I get away with
A FANNY PACK?
Never.
Unless you are
a professional makeup
artist and you require
one to hold your tools.
If not, NO.

Can I get away with
A FEDORA?
Absolutely.
Just make sure your hair
looks good when you whip it off.
Wear it angled slightly forward
and tipped jauntily to one side.
Shoulder-length or longer
hair looks best.

Can I get away with
A VINTAGE BROOCH?
Absolutely.
Pin it to the lapel of a work
blazer or use it to clasp a
fine-knit cardigan. Stylists pin
the cardigan just slightly
off-center (much cooler than
right in the middle).

Can I get away with
A BASEBALL CAP?
It depends.
If you're enjoying
a sports game at a stadium
or jogging, a cap is okay.
Other times, no.

Can I get away with
OVER-THE-KNEE BOOTS?
It depends.
Yes, when paired with skinny
jeans and a top that covers your
bum. No if you're petite—you
risk looking like Puss in Boots.

Can I get away with
A COWBOY HAT?
Never.
I don't care if you're at
a rodeo or on a beach.
It looks horribly cliched.
Sorry.

CONFESSIONS
FROM THE CONFIDENTIAL
FASHION FILES

The obsession with designer shoes is hard to beat in Manhattan. The Manolo Blahnik sample sale in New York City, where fashion editors are invited to buy at below wholesale prices, is not for the faint of heart. (It's akin to a well-dressed rugby scrum.) This is when well-respected, normally sedate and highly sophisticated editors bare razor-sharp elbows while wildly ripping open bags of Manolo heels and clawing their way through piles of thigh-high boots. By 7am, it's packed. The fashionistas all have slightly desperate and ready-to-kill expressions, and we're all kept in a "holding pen" until deemed important enough to enter the sample sale salon itself. Then, the complete chaos begins. The last time I risked shopping at this particularly dangerous brand of sample sale, I scored an overly trendy still-heinously-priced pair of lace booties that drew considerable attention to my chunky calves. I ended up bequeathing them to my stunning Heart Pendant-shaped friend instead, who looks sensational in them.

THE PRETTY TRUTH

RIDICULOUSLY FLAWLESS SKIN AND GORGEOUS HAIR

Take it from me, there's absolutely nothing natural about the "natural" look. You'd be astonished at how plain-looking even universally recognized supermodels are devoid of their lipstick and concealer. But if you want to look slimmer, younger, and prettier right now, learning the insider secrets to great makeup and hair will get you there.

While it's fun to keep on top of the latest, greatest breakthroughs and lavishly expensive lotions and potions, you probably already own products that can give you the same results. Don't fall for the bold-faced claims of the newest wonder products. Makeup brands play brilliantly to our insecurities, alleging to solve problems you never even knew you had. (Do your bottom lashes really need their own mascara?) The amount of products out there is dizzying, and even professionals like myself have a hard time keeping up.

And let's not forget about your hair. Do you deal with an endless array of straighteners, relaxers, flatirons, conditioners, or curl-treatment cocktails to achieve dazzlingly divine hair? Exhausting, right? This chapter is going to cut through the clutter for you. Here you'll find years of insider knowledge…

…AND THE MOST USEFUL BEAUTY SECRETS YOU'VE EVER READ.

CLEANSER

SHOULD I BUY THE HYPE?

No. There are far too many cleansers out there claiming outrageous things that you need a PhD to truly understand. Bottom line: you just need a gentle cleanser to take off your makeup and the daily grime. Good ol' fashioned Cetaphil Daily Facial Cleanser is a dermatologist's secret. Since you're rinsing cleanser off anyway, spend your money on a skin-plumping moisturizer instead of a fancy face wash. (Yes, everything your mum told you about taking off your makeup every night is true.)

DID YOU KNOW?

Look for visuals on packaging to indicate how long you can use a product once it's opened. (6M means you should throw the product out after 6 months.)

MOISTURIZER

DO I REALLY NEED THE EXPENSIVE STUFF?

No, no, and NO again. Brands spend billions on luxurious, lavish packaging to seduce you into parting with your last dollar under the vain promise of youthful skin. All you need to know is this: keep your skin hydrated, work on rebuilding collagen, and be fanatical about using sunblock every single day (even on cloudy days). Focus on holding onto (or recapturing) your skin's youthful volume by boosting elasticity and skin-plumping collagen. Products that will help: Olay Regenerist Wrinkle Revolution Complex, Clinique Repairwear Uplifting Firming Cream, or the deliciously inexpensive Good Skin Lab's Filextra Facial Revolumizing Treatment, which helps stimulate your skin's natural hylauronic acid and collagen production.

Another daily product that makes a huge difference (minus the price tag) is Boots No. 7 Protect & Perfect Intense Beauty Serum. People are obsessed with it in the UK, where they sell one every few seconds. This rich, super intensive formula with antioxidants and firming peptides (fancy words that basically mean it protects and perfects fine lines and wrinkles) is one of the best over-the-counter anti-aging serums on the market.

INSIDE SCOOP

You don't need to use the same brand of cleanser, moisturizer, and eye cream. Mix and match, just make sure they don't all contain harsh ingredients, like salicylic acid or alpha-hydroxy acid, or you may unintentionally cause redness or irritation. And don't waste a dime on toner. A good cleanser is all you need.

EYE CREAM

SHOULD I BOTHER WITH IT?

Some derms say it's not worth it or that it can be too heavy for the delicate eye area. However, an eye cream will hydrate, moisturize, and allow any concealer to smooth on more easily over dark circles. The makeup artists' best way to apply it? Use your ring finger and pat it lightly around the entire eye area. My personal fave is the non-pricey Boots No. 7 Protect & Perfect Intense Eye Cream. If you want to camouflage dark circles, go for a light-reflecting and ultrahydrating cream like Good Skin Lab's Eyliplex-2 or Shiseido's White Lucent Anti-Dark Circles Eye Cream. For puffiness look for anti-inflammatory ingredients like chamomile, cucumber, or aloe and skin-tightening caffeine.

ANTI-AGING

WHAT REALLY WORKS?

I have yet to meet a derm who doesn't swear by a bit of vitamin A derivative (like retinol or retinoic acid) at night to promote skin cell turnover and reduce fine lines. Recognized as the gold standard for anti-aging, it stimulates collagen production, helps reduce hyperpigmentation, and encourages more radiant skin. (You'll need to see your derm for a prescription.)

However, it can be drying and irritating to sensitive skin, so use a pea-sized blob once or twice a week only, or look for milder OTC versions like Vichy LiftActiv Retinol HA Night Total Wrinkle Plumping Care or RoC Retinol Correxion Deep Wrinkle Night Cream (a celeb derm favorite).

THE SIMPLEST SKIN CARE REGIME EVER

CLEANSER

+

MOISTURIZER

+

SUNSCREEN

(even when it's cloudy)

CONCEALER

WHAT'S SO GREAT ABOUT CONCEALER?

A small dab of the right shade is like a magic wand, swiping away dark circles, small areas of redness, and any imperfections. The wrong shade does the opposite—making you look older and drawing attention to any problem areas. To get the right color, test-drive shades on the blue veins of your hand. (Yellow-based shades work on most skin tones, so leave the pinks and greens to the pros.) And your skin is drier and paler in winter, so adjust your shade accordingly. To camouflage dark under-eye circles, look for a yellow-based shade, which will counteract deep red or purple, and apply with your fingers. Try a combo of YSL's Touche Éclat followed by a dab of Clé de Peau Concealer. This concealer is creamy enough to cover any humdinger of a pimple, yet whisper-light-enough to blend away dark circles.

WHAT'S THE BEST WAY TO APPLY?

Apply concealer after your eye cream so that it blends more easily, and always apply in natural lighting. Don't use a magnifying mirror, as it's easy to be heavy-handed.

HOW DO I CONCEAL A HUGE PIMPLE?

On the set, when celebs show up with a close-up-destroying angry red blob, makeup artists rely on these two insider tricks: a drop of Visine to remove any redness and an aspirin mashed up with water dabbed on with a Q-tip to reduce inflammation. Pat on concealer with a small brush and blend in small circles around the offending enemy. For darker skin tones, use a medium to dark concealer and a light tapping motion to "break up" any discoloration.

WHAT ABOUT PUFFY EYES?

Here's how makeup artists deal with hard-partying celebs who show up with puffy eyes: Put two spoons in the freezer, then place under eyes to reduce swelling. Or use a compress: Talika's Eye Decompress is an antioxidant-rich, travel-friendly eye mask that refreshes and decongests swollen skin in minutes. A concealer with a soothing eye roller works, too: Garnier's Skin Renew Anti-Dark-Circle Roller has caffeine and lemon essence to brighten under-eye skin.

FOUNDATION

OR TINTED MOISTURIZER OR BB CREAM

HOW DO I CHOOSE THE RIGHT ONE?

First of all, don't bother with foundation if you've got good skin. If you feel you need more than concealer, the next best thing is a tinted moisturizer. Makeup artists swear by Laura Mercier's Tinted Moisturizer or BB creams, which even out skin tone while camouflaging dark spots and imperfections. Can't live without foundation? Find one that doesn't look mask-like or as if it's sitting on top of your skin. Test it in daylight—it should disappear completely.

Smooth streaks in two or three shades from the side of your cheek down to your jawline. Some brands separate by "pink-based" or "yellow-based." A rule of thumb: If you tend to burn in the sun, you're pink-based; if you tan relatively easily, you're likely to have yellow undertones. Can't test before you buy? Bring a shade that's worked in the past and find one that's a close match. Most drugstores offer generous return policies for makeup; just keep your receipt in case it turns out to be the wrong shade.

INSIDE SCOOP

Forget fancy brushes and apply foundation using your fingers or a damp makeup sponge. Makeup artists use the "stippling" technique: a soft dabbing motion in small circles across the face, so that the foundation blends into the skin to look natural and translucent.

FINISHING

HOW CAN I BE SHINE-FREE ALL DAY?

Set your makeup with a light dusting of skin-brightening pressed powder to keep your face shine-free throughout the day. An industry favorite is T. LeClerc's Pressed Powder in Banane—it looks alarmingly yellow in the compact, but truly makes skin look lit from within. I discovered it when I lived in Paris, and have since hunted it down in the U.S. Want to avoid powder altogether? Makeup artists carry Shiseido's Pureness Oil-Control Blotting Paper to use on their clients' shiny T-zones.

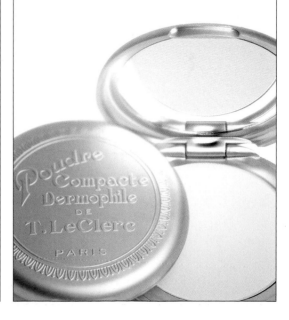

BLUSH

HOW DO I GET A ROSY GLOW?

The idea is to create a glow that looks like it's coming from under your skin. In general, light peach and pinkish shades work best for fairer skin tones, apricot hues for olive complexions, and plum looks prettiest on dark skin.

HOW DO I PICK A FORMULA?

If you have oily skin, a powder blush will absorb any excess grease. For dry skin, a more emollient cream blush will blend most easily. Allow any moisturizer to soak in thoroughly before applying so that the blush doesn't streak. Cheek stains and gels can be tricky to master and blend (especially on very dry skin) but they do give that glorious first-kiss flush.

Combination skin can use both formulations: Go for a creamy blush (like Stila Convertible Color) in winter and a powder blush in the summer (NARS Blush in Orgasm lives up to its name by making you look like you've just had a romp in the bedroom). For a stain, makeup artists swear by the virtually undetectable Benefit's Benetint.

BRONZER

HOW CAN I FAKE A TAN IN THE DEAD OF WINTER?

Pick a bronzer that's no more than two shades darker than your complexion and use a fluffy, oversized bronzer brush to dust it where the sun would naturally hit—on your forehead, down your nose, and on the apples of your cheeks. For fair-to-medium skin, try a peach-based bronzer like Guerlain's Terracotta Bronzing Powder, while olive skin tones might try something more brown-based like NARS's Bronzing Powder in Laguna, or Physicians Formula Baked Bronzer in Baked Bronze. Makeup artists add a dab of pink blush just on the apples of the cheeks over the top of bronzer for a believably natural glow.

INSIDE SCOOP

A cotton wool ball works just as well for applying blush as an expensive blusher brush. Got too much color on your cheeks? Dust a translucent powder over the top to blend out any heavy-handed mistakes.

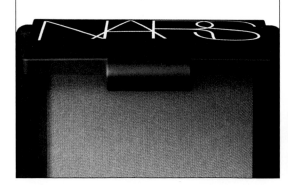

LIPSTICK

HOW DO I WEAR IT AND NOT LOOK TOO MADE UP?

Get a warm shade that's one shade darker than your natural lip color. (Try to match the shade to your gum color.) Sheer formulas are goof-proof since a less precise application is needed to give that fresh-faced look. Try Clinique's Almost Lipstick, a super sheer wash of color in iconic Black Honey (every makeup artist carries it) or a pretty pink that suits everyone, like Flirty Honey.

CAN ANYONE PULL OFF A RED LIP?

A good rule of thumb: The darker your skin, the warmer the red should be. If you're nervous about a bold red lipstick, try a sheer gloss or tone it down by layering with a beigey shade. Got very fair skin? Swipe on some bronzer so you don't look washed out. And a red lip is a useful beauty trick to distract from any unwanted redness in your face, bringing the focus to your pout instead. If you want to make your teeth look whiter without a professional whitening treatment, a blue-toned red lipstick helps counteract any yellow.

LIPLINER

LINER OR NO LINER?

Up to you. Just make sure there is no visible line. Lip liner should help your lipstick stay on and create a border for your lips. Choose one that matches your lips, not the lipstick. Makeup artists never try to create a dramatically different shape (no clown lips, please!) and just use it to correct and fill in the lipline where needed. When applying liner don't use the point of the pencil and instead use the side to make short strokes along the natural lipline. MAC's Lip Pencil in Spice or Whirl are the industry standards for nude liners that work on just about everyone.

WHAT ABOUT LIP PRIMER?

Nah. Not worth it. The newest formulas have longer-lasting pigment, so you don't need a primer.

INSIDE SCOOP

Smooth your smoocher: Brush gently over your lips at night with a toothbrush and rub on a rich balm. Good ol' Aquaphor Lip Repair gets the job done, or I stock up on the best-kept Australian beauty secret, Lucas' Papaw Ointment, a thick, emollient gel which is the solution to practically everything.

EYE SPY

4 SIMPLE STEPS
TO AN EVERYDAY LOOK FOR EYE SHADOW

PRIME YOUR EYELIDS
so that your shadow stays on. I can't live without Urban Decay
Eyeshadow Primer Potion, which makes any brand of eye shadow last an eternity.
I have "butter lids," so without primer, any shadow disappears within minutes.

APPLY A LIGHT SHADE ALL OVER YOUR LID
from the lash line up to the brow. This should be a shade or two lighter
than your skin tone to rejuvenate the eye.

BRUSH A SLIGHTLY DARKER SHADE
ALONG THE CREASE LINE
to create definition and depth. Pick a crease color that mimics
one of the darker tones of your iris. Use the same dark shade to
line the upper lash line as a subtle liner.

ADD A BONE-COLORED SHADE
just under the brow and blend so that there are no hard edges.

SHADOW

For everyday wear, choose a palette of flattering neutrals, then emphasize your individual eye shade with this makeup artist insider secret: look for the contrasting shade that instantly makes your eyes look brighter, fresher, and younger. Here's how…

If your eyes are…

BLUE

Make your eyes sparkle like sapphires with complimentary shades:

PEACH · TAUPE · PLUM · BROWN

The shade that gives you WOW FACTOR:

BRONZE

GREEN

Make your eyes glisten like emeralds with complimentary shades:

GOLDEN LIME · OLIVE · KHAKI GREEN

The shade that gives you WOW FACTOR:

PURPLE

BROWN

Bring out the rich mahogany tones with complimentary shades:

SANDY BEIGE · CARAMEL · RICH CHOCOLATE

The shade that gives you WOW FACTOR:

GREEN

HAZEL

Bring out the golden sparkle with complimentary shades:

SHEER ROSE · WARM TAUPE · CHESTNUT BROWN

The shade that gives you WOW FACTOR:

PINK

EYE SPY

EYELINER

WHAT DO I DO IF I REALLY CAN'T DRAW A STRAIGHT LINE?

Don't bother trying to be precise. The secret is to dot and wiggle the liner between your upper lashes so the effect is a full, thicker lash line and not an obvious, harsh line. If you're new to liner, apply with an angled eyeliner brush dipped into dark eye shadow, which creates softly defined eyes. And even though waterproof liner sounds slightly alarming (what if it never comes off?), it just means that it has an ingenious long-lasting formula that won't smudge. One of the best smudge-proof eyeliners? Crayon Khôl Terrybly Color Eye Pencil By Terry goes on as smoothly as a cream and stays put for eight hours, but washes right off with makeup remover.

CAN I STOP MY LINER FROM SMUDGING?

I learned this trick backstage from a famous makeup artist: Trace over pencil liner with a fine brush dipped in a matching powder shadow (MAC Pencil Brush 219 is a good one) to keep it in place all day.

INSIDE SCOOP

This is an invaluable TV trick I learned decades ago: Make eyes look brighter by lining the inner rims with a nude (not white, eek! Scary!) liner. Try NARS Larger Than Life Long-Wear Eyeliner in Rue Bonaparte (a barely-there nude) or Make Up For Ever Concealer & Lip Liner Pencil (it says it's for lips, but it's super creamy) in No.100.

LASH CURLERS

HOW TO MAKE YOUR EYES LOOK BIGGER THAN THEY REALLY ARE

Invest in an eyelash curler. Curl your lashes before you apply mascara and watch as it magically opens up your eyes. It might sound scary, but once you practice a few times, it's worth the extra step. Shiseido's eyelash curlers have a very lightly curved base so they can get incredibly close to the lash roots. On short lashes pinch the curler three times at the base, opening and closing it to make sure you capture every one of your lashes.

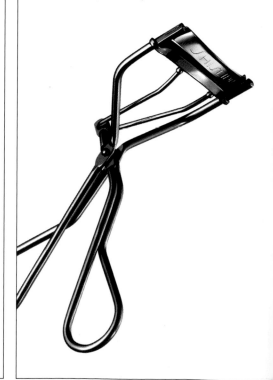

MASCARA

FATTEN UP

Go for a volumizing mascara and look for oversized, Christmas tree–like brushes that deposit the most amount of mascara onto the base of your lashes and then brush it all the way through to the tips.

PUT IT ON LIKE A PRO

Hold a small mirror at your chin and tilt your head back slightly. Wedge the brush right under the base of your top lashes, then wiggle the wand along the base of the lash line, before drawing it upward to the tips. Apply two coats (the more mascara, the thicker the lashes) and then double-coat just the outer lashes so they look thicker, fuller, and help open up your eyes.

TAKE IT OFF

The number one reason women don't buy waterproof mascara is that they hate getting it off. Me too. In Paris, I discovered Lierac's Diopti Démaq Gentle Eye Makeup Remover (find it at the drugstore) that, when dabbed onto a cotton pad, easily removes even the hardiest Tammy Faye–worthy waterproof mascara.

FALSE LASHES

THE EASIEST WAY EVER TO PUT ON FALSE LASHES

Put mascara on and cut the false lash strip in half. Forget the individual lashes—too complicated—leave them to the pros. Dab a tiny blob of black lash glue (the white glue will turn colorless, but isn't black easier?) along the strip and wait a few seconds for them to dry. Hold the lash strip with one hand and place it along the top outer edge of your eye. Allow the glue to dry slightly and gently press the base of the lashes into place. Fluttery, sexy lashes in seconds.

SO, WHICH ONES?

Revlon Fantasy Lengths self-adhesive lashes are goof-proof to apply. Vincent Longo Lash Tips are already cut to half-length and are one-third the length of regular lashes. (I mean, who has time to find scissors these days?)

HOW TO SCORE THE PERFECT HAIRCUT

Reluctant to go under the knife in order to look younger?
Head to a hairdresser instead. Celebs have known for decades
that a flattering cut can make you look years younger
and infinitely better. And why wouldn't you want to look thinner
and prettier with just the flutter of a pair of skilled shears?

The three things your stylist needs to know about you:

WHAT YOU LIKE

Love Jennifer Aniston's hair? Don't we all. But unless your own hair is a similar texture and length and her face shape resembles yours, it might not be possible to get the exact same look with your hair. Bring in tons of pictures of styles that you like to spark a discussion about a version of that particular cut that will work best for you.

HOW MUCH TIME YOU (HONESTLY) HAVE

If you're a wash-and-go kind of girl, don't point to anything that requires major styling effort. Are you in a frantic hurry every morning getting the kids out the door? Or do you have plenty of leisure time to spare with a hair dryer? Either way, your cut has to work with your daily lifestyle.

HOW SHORT YOU'RE WILLING TO GO

Your idea of "just a trim, please" may be entirely different from your scissor-happy stylist's. Using your fingers, show him the shortest length you'll consider. If you're super nervous about cutting off too much, ask your stylist to straighten your hair first and cut it dry, since it will be easier to tell the exact length it will be.

DON'T GET STUCK IN A RUT.

Sorry, but you can't get away with the same hairstyle you've
had since you were twelve and not look dated, so ask
your stylist if they think your cut is still the best one for you. He might
suggest something a bit softer or more sophisticated.
Get a few tweaks to your cut each time you visit the salon for
a trim for a simple way to refresh your look.

DON'T WEAR YOUR HAIR TOO LONG.

Hair that's too long can make you look old. Period.
A perennially elegant cut is one that grazes the collarbone
(or just above), gives your hair plenty of youthful
volume, and doesn't drag down your features.

DON'T LET ANYONE NEAR YOU WITH A RAZOR.

Especially if you've got super fine hair. Razor cuts take away
precious, much-needed volume.

DON'T GO FOR BANGS UNLESS YOU ARE CERTAIN.

Unless you know you have the time to style bangs to look neat,
and your face shape can carry them off (long bangs can make
a small forehead look even tinier), know that cutting bangs
is a major style commitment.

DON'T GO FOR A BLUNT CUT.

Unless you have a slender, chiseled face that can
carry off such a severe style.

THE RIGHT HAIR COLOR

BLONDE

WHAT YOU NEED TO KNOW

Going blonde can be tricky business, so enlist a pro when stripping your hair of pigment. In winter, have your colorist make you go brighter; in summer, liven up bleached, parched hair by adding youthful golden or honey tones that reflect the light. Don't go for one-dimensional, ashy-blonde shades that wash you out; opt for flattering high- and lowlights of various blonde shades. In the sun, prevent dulling and discoloration with a UV protection spray. Try Pureology Essential Repair ColourMax, a lightweight UV filter spray that repairs distressed hair and gives color protection and shine. A final word: If you're going lighter, be prepared to alter your makeup to include paler, sheer shades that won't look so harsh.

BRUNETTE

WHAT YOU NEED TO KNOW

Even the deepest brunettes can benefit from subtle highlights that act like a brightening agent by adding color to your skin and making you look more sun-kissed. This is for my brunette girls, as you can easily look washed-out. Lighten up with bright caramels or rich chestnut, but avoid aging ashy tones. For highlights, keep within one or two shades of your natural color—no skunk stripes or 1980s frosting, please. And forget the of-the-moment dark-to-light-ombre trend unless you're in your twenties. Great news: it's easy for brunettes' hair to look super shiny, as brown reflects the light, and face-framing highlights will distract from any imperfections like dark under-eye circles.

REDHEAD

WHAT YOU NEED TO KNOW

Yes, you'll turn heads and the shade will bring out gorgeous emerald-green eyes, but red is also the hair color that's the hardest to maintain. Commit to three-to-four-week touch-ups to keep its vibrancy (which can be a pricey investment). The general rule is this: Don't go red unless you naturally have those tones in your hair. If you're a true redhead and are tempted by highlights, keep them subtle so you don't lose the intensity of your natural color. Last word of warning: Don't overuse color-depositing shampoos— they can turn your stunning color into an unsightly fuchsia shade.

{
INSIDE SCOOP

Want lower-maintenance color? Ask for highlights that peek out from underneath and inside your hair, instead of right on the top of your head. They look especially cute when your hair is up in a ponytail. And as they grow out, they'll be far less maintenance. Or part your hair slightly differently until your next appointment so your roots are less obvious.
}

GRAY

WHAT YOU NEED TO KNOW

Unless it's a conscious fashion decision and you can truly pull it off, don't go gray since (obviously) it can make you look older than you are. Covering your roots is the most non-invasive and effective anti-aging solution on the planet. If you don't want to see a pro, try a simple root touch-up: Clairol Root Touch-up works in just ten minutes and lasts up to three weeks. Celebrity colorist to just about every superstar, Rita Hazan Root Concealer for Gray Coverage comes in five shades and lasts until you wash it out. But what if you want to embrace your gray? Remember to use a shampoo that's specifically formulated to keep it brilliant and cut out any yellow (Clairol Shimmer Lights Blonde & Silver Shampoo is a good one) and keep clothing and makeup more youthful so you make your hair color a style statement.

LEAVE COLOR
TO THE PROS

IF YOU HAVE A BIG EVENT
AND CAN'T AFFORD FOR IT
TO GO HORRIBLY WRONG.

IF YOU'RE PLANNING
ON A DRASTIC
HAIR COLOR CHANGE.

IF YOUR HAIR IS
CHEMICALLY TREATED
(PERMED, RELAXED,
STRAIGHTENED)
OR DAMAGED.

IF YOU'RE GOING BLONDER,
OR ADDING HIGHLIGHTS
FOR THE FIRST TIME.

COLOR-KEEPING
SECRETS

Your hair color is only as good as the condition of your hair, so get regular trims and use a shampoo and conditioner specifically formulated for color-treated hair. Why invest in pricey hair color and then wash it away with regular shampoos that have too much detergent? Use a super gentle baby shampoo or look for sulfate-free options. Invest in a better conditioner than shampoo since you leave it on your hair longer. Celebrity colorists swear by Kérastase Masquintense, a weekly deep-conditioning hair mask that keeps your color salon-fresh.

INSIDE SCOOP

Oops! Decided to save money and do it at home, but it's gone too dark or too brassy? Try this insider trick: Comb a teaspoon of warm olive oil through damp hair and let it sit for a few minutes. The oil will loosen up your overzealous dye job from the hair cuticle.

HAIR COLORING TIPS

DON'T GO FOR A COLOR CHANGE THAT'S MORE THAN A FEW SHADES AWAY FROM YOUR ROOTS.

HELP YOUR COLORIST.

A picture is worth a thousand words. "I don't want brassy," means very different things to different people and is deeply confusing to a professional colorist who spends hours mixing up complicated hair shades. Show your colorist a picture.

BE REALISTIC.

Don't ask for Marilyn Monroe blonde if you really can't afford the constant upkeep. If you're considering going red you need to commit to touch-ups every three to four weeks.

BEAR IN MIND WHAT WILL SUIT YOUR PROFESSION OR PERSONALITY.

If you have a conservative profession, a crazy wacky hair color probably won't do much for your promotion prospects.

CONSIDERING A MAJOR HAIR COLOR CHANGE?

Only go to a reputable salon with a recommendation from someone whose hair color you love.

ALWAYS COLOR AFTER YOUR CUT.

A professional colorist will frame your hair color around the cut, making your new style look its absolute best.

HAIR DONE

NOT YOUR BORING PONYTAIL

This is my go-to day three hairdo. Just add height at the crown by teasing your roots and pull hair back into a high, tight ponytail. Secure the ponytail with a band (Goody has a range that matches any hair color) and then use your fingers to pull the hair up just above the band to create more volume at the crown. Finally, wrap a few strands of your hair around the band to cover it even more, and finish with hairspray. Add a sparkling hair accessory to dress it up. And the best part? Less washing and fewer blowouts, and you'll still look fabulous.

INSIDE SCOOP

Apply styling products while hair is slightly damp. Too dry, and the product won't blend evenly through your hair.

THE EASIEST CHIGNON EVER

Part hair and pull into a low ponytail. Twirl hair and spin it into a tight coil, then twist it around the base. Tuck in the ends and stick in old-fashioned U-shaped hairpins that hold more hair than skinny bobby pins. Use a strong-hold hairspray to keep flyaways at bay.

TRIM BANGS AT HOME IN A PINCH

Take really small (and I mean really small) sections of your bangs, hold each section with one hand two inches from the bottom, then snip slowly into that section of bangs at an upward-slanted angle.

MAKE YOUR PRICEY SALON BLOWOUT LAST

Ask for conditioner at the ends only and for a light volumizing spray at the roots. But the real secret weapon when you're back at home? A dry shampoo the next morning, like Oscar Blandi Pronto Dry Shampoo that revives unwashed hair and restores major volume.

BROWS SHOULD BE TWO SHADES DARKER
THAN YOUR HAIR COLOR.

FULLER EYEBROWS MAKE
YOUR FACE LOOK SLIMMER
AND GIVE YOUR EYES MORE DEFINITION.

SHORT EYEBROWS MAKE YOUR
EYES LOOK SMALLER AND YOUR NOSE FATTER.

DON'T CREATE TOO MUCH OF AN ARCH—
THE WICKED STEPMOTHER LOOK
IS NEVER A GOOD ONE.

PLUCK IN NATURAL DAYLIGHT,
SO YOU CAN REALLY SEE
WHAT'S GOING ON.

BRUSH BROWS AND SET THEM
IN PLACE WITH A CLEAR BROW GEL.

NOTES ON FRAGRANCE

HOW DO I TEST THEM?

Shop in the morning, since it's when your sense of smell is keenest, and test no more than two scents at a time or you risk overwhelming your nose. Dab aromas on the outer part of your wrists rather than the insides, which can pick up oils and odors from everyday tasks.

HOW DO I CHOOSE A SUMMER FRAGRANCE?

Body and outdoor temperatures amplify fragrance, so go for fresh floral or crisp citrus notes that wear well in the hot and humid months.

WHERE SHOULD I PUT IT?

Dab it onto the spots where your body collects heat, like the crooks of your elbows, knees, your cleavage, or behind your ears. Applied too much? Dilute the scent by applying an unscented cream or lotion.

WILL IT EXPIRE?

Fragrances have an average life span of approximately three years. (Lighter, fresher citrus and florals tend to have a shorter life span, while the richer, woody or oriental fragrances last longer.) And heat and light are perfume's worst enemies, so prolong your favorite one by storing it out of direct sunlight or in the refrigerator.

CLASSICS TO TRY

MARNI
An ethereal spicy fragrance with notes of eclectic, raw wood.

CHANEL CHANCE
A youthful, fresh floral.

MICHAEL KORS SIGNATURE
A fruity, honeylike white flower.

COACH POPPY
A sparkling, vibrant fruity floral.

DONNA KARAN WOMAN
Sandalwood and Haitian vetiver with creamy notes of orange flower.

INSIDE SCOOP

Know which scents men find the most attractive? Woody and clean scents with notes of citrus and/or lavender.

CONFESSIONS
FROM THE CONFIDENTIAL FASHION FILES

I have so many confessions for this chapter, I thought I'd just spill everything at once. First, let me share with you my brow horror story. When I lived in Hong Kong I was about to shoot a live TV show with a famous Hollywood heart-throb when, moments before I was scheduled to appear in the studio, an aesthetician mistakenly swiped off the entire half of one of my brows during a particularly overzealous waxing session. "Who needs brows anyway?" I jovially comforted the horrified aesthetician.

And then, one Thanksgiving morning I thought it would be a great idea to go from my natural blonde dishwater hair color to a deep aubergine color. "Happy Tha–What happened to your hair?" stammered the hostess, as she threw open the door to a packed crowd and I spotted my ex-boyfriend's new girlfriend stifle a giggle.

Regretfully, that blunder reminded me of the time I spotted a sign for "Hair, Special Offer" and rushed unknowingly into an African American hair-braiding salon, then sat awkwardly while the stylist practiced blonde highlights for the first time ever.

But my most humiliating confession is my concealer story. This chapter brought back painful memorics of the time I was in Havana, Cuba, for a professional salsa dance invitational (another story, another time) and swiped on a now-thankfully-discontinued light-reflecting concealer under my eyes. "What's wrong with her face?" I heard a few confused Cuban audience members mutter as I swirled, oblivious, around the dance floor. The circa-1980s strobe lights had transformed my under-eye concealer into glow-in-the-dark warrior stripes.

A FINAL WORD ON WOW

CONGRATULATIONS MY DARLING, YOU'VE GOT THE WOW FACTOR!
You did it! It was a wild journey, but now you're totally, completely, without a doubt armed with everything you need to look truly amazing. You've glimpsed behind the scenes of the smoke-and-mirrors fashion industry, and you know what's real and what's fake, fake, fake. You know the tips and tricks to look your absolute best.

You've learned to use your body type as your guide when shopping, and how to interpret the trends to make them work for your lifestyle, shape, and budget. You have the confidence, grace, and poise that WOW FACTOR! women bring into a room, and everyone around you is going to feel it, too. You can pair accessories, shop, and even apply eyeliner like a pro. So my hope now is that you're fully equipped to walk into a store, get ready for a party, or get dressed in the morning with complete and utter confidence.

...AND IF YOU EVER FEEL YOUR WOW IS SLIPPING, JUST FLIP BACK THROUGH THE BOOK TO REDISCOVER THE BEST *YOU* AGAIN.

MOVING ON

So, by now, with your newly trained eye, you might be looking at your closet and realizing it's probably a good time for a quick sort-though. Let's take everything out, and only put back what looks (and makes you feel!) sensational. It's very liberating, and best done on a dull, rainy day. After you've done that, here are a few suggestions for what you can do with all your decidedly non-WOWfits:

CONSIGN THEM

Call ahead to a consignment store near you, and ask which season they are interested in taking inventory. (Don't waste time hauling flimsy summer shifts in the dead of winter; they probably won't accept them.) Most stores require dry-cleaned pieces without missing buttons or zips that need to be fixed. Many prefer designer brands, but if you have timeless pieces in good condition, they may be interested in them as well.

SELL THEM ONLINE

If you're planning on selling everything online, it's easiest to sell things in their current season. You'll have a better chance off-loading your cozy knits in winter, and skimpy T-shirts in summer.

DONATE THEM

Want to do some good? Donate to your local Salvation Army or a homeless shelter. (I once donated a giant stack of clothing to a local shelter, and for weeks spotted several grandmas walking around in my sequined boleros.)

SWAP THEM WITH YOUR FRIENDS

Invite your friends over for wine, cheese, and "shopping." Make an evening out of it, and encourage everyone to bring along some of their own things that are in great shape but perhaps wrong for their body type, or aren't a shade that works for them. One woman's trash (like an expensive hip-hugging red dress she can't bring herself to toss away) will surely be another woman's treasure.

HOOKED ON WOW?

Dying to know more? Not to worry, I'm not going to leave
you stranded. If you've still got more questions, I would love
for us to continue this fabulous conversation online at

JACQUISTAFFORD.COM

Here, you can stay up-to-the-minute on the latest and greatest
style tips, plus I'll give you your own, completely personalized
WOW assessment. You can e-mail me a photo of yourself, and I'll
help you determine your body shape and offer practical suggestions
about exactly what to buy from your favorite stores. (Like having
a pocket version of me with you when you go shopping!) On the
site, you can also sign up for one of my powerful "Body Shape
Workshops" in an area near you, and come to meet me in person
so we can have a good old chat. You'll receive my weekly newsletter
packed with really useful insider style tips that are specifically catered
to you. From live podcasts to detailed web seminars, I'll answer
every one of your burning style questions. And the best part? You
can even sign up for a one-on-one. Like a fashion fairy godmother,
I'll show up (poof!) at a store near you, and help you look like a
million dollars (without you having to spend it!). Yes, my darlings,
I can't wait to meet you and uncover your WOW together.

20 RULES THAT WOW! WOMEN LIVE BY

So, here's what I'd like you to remember forever.
Actually, if you remember nothing at all from the rest of this book,
these should be your **EVERY-MORNING MANTRAS:**

1

CONFIDENCE
is the hottest
accessory
you can own.

2

**SIZE MEANS
NOTHING.**
Fit is everything.

3

**DON'T LEAVE HOME
WITHOUT GREAT
ACCESSORIES.**

4

STAY TRUE TO YOUR OWN BODY SHAPE.
Don't fall back into old habits and buy clothes that don't flatter
your figure. Only love clothes that love you back!

5

**YOU DON'T HAVE TO BE RICH
OR SKINNY TO LOOK AMAZING.**
Trust me, there are plenty of rich and skinny women
who look dreadful. People look fabulous simply
because they dress for the best version of themselves.

6

**STAY "IN-THE-KNOW"
BUT DON'T FOLLOW
TRENDS LIKE A SLAVE.**
Show the world that you're
hip to what's hot in fashion, but
you've adapted the trends to suit
your body, age, and lifestyle.
(Everyone will think you know
something they don't.)

7

**NEVER SHOP
WITHOUT A PLAN.**
Make a list of what
you need and stick to it
(regardless of what's on
sale). And think in terms
of whole outfits.

8

**GIVE YOUR HAIR
A TRIM EVERY
SIX TO EIGHT
WEEKS,**
and your closet a trim
every season.

9

**DON'T UNDERESTIMATE
THE POWER OF THE
PERFECT BRA.**
Getting it right will make you
look younger, thinner, and sexier.

11 HAVING MUST-HAVE PIECES FOR YOUR BODY SHAPE in your closet means never having to complain "I have nothing to wear," again.

12 DON'T WASTE TIME WAITING TO ACHIEVE THE PERFECT BODY. Make the one that you've got right now look amazing.

10 EMBRACE A SENSE OF HUMOR. I laugh heartily at my old "fat pics." We're only human and there's no such thing as perfect.

13 NEVER LEAVE HOME WITHOUT LIP GLOSS. (Or at least concealer.)

14 THE FIRST RULE TO LOOKING REALLY WEALTHY is sleek, shiny hair and a clear complexion.

15 THERE IS NO SUCH THING AS "TOO OLD FOR STYLE."

16 KNOWING WHAT TO WEAR UNDER YOUR CLOTHES is just as crucial as what you wear on top.

17 THERE ARE LIMITLESS STYLE POSSIBILITIES IN YOUR CLOSET. Don't restrict your options: A dull pair of "work pants" can be worn at night with a silky cami under a blazer. (See? More clothes, less spending.)

18 THE SECOND RULE TO LOOKING WEALTHY is about killer shoes and a beyond-fabulous handbag.

19 BE YOURSELF, not someone else's idea of who to be. So obvious, but so many women forget.

20 EVERY DAY IS A NEW OPPORTUNITY TO BE FABULOUS.

THANK YOU!

COULDN'T HAVE DONE IT WITHOUT YOU

A particular shout out
(in print forever, no less!)
to the people I adore…

Rob Lopez—my rock, my partner, my everything. You put up with my tantrums and meltdowns, and you're my world. Charlotte and I are so lucky to have you.

My agent, Kim Perel, without whom I'd never have gathered all these insights together in the first place (and who is, without a doubt, the hardest working agent and writer known to mankind)…

Susannah Howard, my supermodel assistant, who was with me from day one, and spent months hunched over her Mac, sourcing images, reading copy, and living and breathing every syllable…

Lauren Marino, my amazingly insightful editor at Penguin, who believed in this project and brought it to life…

Bonnie Siegler, Jessica Bloom, Emily Karian, Lucy Andersen, and the ingenious creative team at Eight and a Half (8point5.com) for turning a plain, typed manuscript into magic, and making each page look more spectacular than I could ever have imagined. They not only designed it, they produced and packaged the whole thing too.

The diligent Claire Jessup, Jordan Webb, Sophie Kennedy, Elizabeth Tuke, and Rachael Smith from the WWW.OUTNET.COM, who uncomplainingly supplied practically every one of the gorgeous clothing images on the pages…

My insider, industry friends for reminding me about super helpful extra nuggets: Megan O'Sullivan on retail secrets, Heather Patt and Brooke Rinehart for their insights on bras, Brooke Axtell for her knowledge on swimwear, Julie Howard for her wisdom on all things beauty…

Kathleen Pierce and Livia Marotta, who were the first friends to offer to get the word out to the world…

Valerie Latona, my dear friend and former boss, who was always there with just the perfect amount of invaluable brilliance on just about everything…

And Mum and Julie (who despite their complete lack of interest in fashion) will no doubt tell anyone who'll listen how FANTASTIC this book is, simply because they're my two biggest fans…

And Daddy—who really taught me everything about how to WOW! Thanks!

AND SPECIAL THANKS TO
Wendy Sherman, Connie Klepper, Brooke Alpert, Dr. Fredric Brandt, Nigel Barker, Kathleen McGraw, Rainy Farrell, Kristen Shaughnessy, Casey Maloney, Allison Hemming, Sally Wadyka, Salih Cakirca, Yesim Cakirca, Nurten Cileli, Laurie Daniel, Mariko Casiano, Ingrid Jones-Suarez, Ying Lam, Marcy Roth, Michele Horner, Nicole Cardillo, Leslie Stevens, Jane Seymour, Michelle Lockhart, Lauren Rich, Wes Boas, Shanon Kogler, Lori Brightman M.D., Nathalie Schueller, Karen Ferko, Alison Brod, Ted Rossi, Kasumi Ito, Marie-Laure Fournier, Nancy Schuster, David Baratta, Heather Carlucci, Nicky Deam, Christine Sforzo, Corynne Corbett, Matthew Owens, Katie Nida-Rovano, Marissa Vitagliano, Marissa Riviello, Elina Kazan, Alison Kmiotek, Sue Tong, Marissa Nicolaescu, Alyssa Bendetson, Cody Howard, Jorge Cruise, Liz Koppelman, and Danielle Kroll.

PHOTO CREDITS

All images of clothing/accessories supplied by The Outnet (OUTNET.COM)
except the following:

18 Ted Rossi clutch
19 Becca by Rebecca Virtue bandeau and pant
20 Rebecca Taylor leopard dress
27 Becca by Rebecca Virtue bandeau and pant
28 Dana-Maxx red dress
34 Giuseppe Zanotti heels
35 Panache bra-sized bikini top and pant
37 Ann Taylor green cardigan
42 DKNY red sweater
43 Aerin Rose one-piece
50 DKNY motorcycle boots
51 Betsey Johnson underwired top and skirted pant
53 Stuart Weitzman boots
Ann Taylor turtleneck
108 Victoria Secret coat
Ann Taylor gloves
Ann Taylor sweater
Deux Lux Felix weekender bag
109 Camilla kaftan
129 Giuseppe Zanotti heels
131 Stuart Weitzman boots
Giuseppe Zanotti pumps
Hanes hosiery
139 Dana-Maxx red top
149 Stuart Weitzman boots
152 Diego Rocha handbag
Mariela Zapata clutch
Stuart Weitzman boots
Stuart Weitzman flats
157 Ann Taylor red dress
160 Accessory Artists cuff
161 Ted Rossi stacked bangles
162 Ann Taylor tan belt
Ann Taylor glitter belt
Ann Taylor yellow belt
163 Stuart Weitzman boots
Pretty Ballerinas ballet flats
166 Kooba handbag
Ted Rossi clutch
169 All sunglasses courtesy of Luxottica
Vogue Eyewear 2757 (Oval face)
Vogue Eyewear 2756 (Square face)
Ray-Ban 3025 (Heart face)
Ray-Ban 2140 (Round face)